THE NOBEL LAUREATES' GUIDE TO
THE SMARTEST TARGETS FOR THE WORLD
2016–2030

Copenhagen Consensus Center and Australia Consensus Centre are think tanks that investigate and publish the best policies and investment opportunities based on data and cost-benefit analysis for governments and philanthropists to make the world a better place. We work with 100+ of the world's top economists and 7 Nobel Laureates to prioritize solutions to the world's biggest problems.

This project has engaged with 82 top economists and 44 sector experts to identify the targets with the greatest benefit-to-cost ratio for the next set of UN development goals. The project has reviewed 107 targets in 100+ peer-reviewed research across more than 20 key areas. Together with several Nobel Laureates it provides the UN and the world with information on costs and benefits for the top global targets.

For more information on our Post-2015 Consensus project, including the content of this book, take a look at post2015consensus.com or contact project manager Brad Wong at brad@copenhagenconsensus.com.

THE NOBEL LAUREATES' GUIDE TO THE SMARTEST TARGETS FOR THE WORLD 2016−2030

Copenhagen Consensus Center USA, Inc.

info@copenhagenconsensus.com
www.copenhagenconsensus.com

Copyright © 2015 by Copenhagen Consensus Center
Cover design by stevieprojects.com

All Rights Reserved.

No part of this book may be reproduced or utilized in any form or by any means, electronic or mechanical, including photocopying, recording, or by any information storage and retrieval system, without permission in writing from the publisher.

Second edition
ISBN 978-1-940003-12-2

CONTENTS

Authors of Post-2015 Consensus Assessment,
Perspective and Viewpoint Papers   vii

How to read this book   1

Introduction – Smarter goals for the UN   3

Post-2015 Targets   19
Overview of Targets   20
1. Air Pollution: Better Stoves Can Reduce Indoor Air Pollution   23
2. Biodiversity: What's Worth Saving?   27
3. Climate Change: It's Time To Give Up The Two Degree Target   31
4. Conflict and Violence: The Economics Of Violence   34
5. Data for Development: Measuring The Next Global Development Goals   38
6. Education: The Trouble With Universal Education   41
7. Energy: How Indoor Stoves Can Help Solve Global Poverty   45
8. Food Security: Build Road In Developing World To Bolster Food Supplies   49
9. Gender Equality: Putting Gender Equality Onto The Post 2015 Development Agenda   52
10. Governance And Institutions: How Can The UN Measure If Better Governance Programs Work?   55
11. Health Systems: Strengthen Health Systems To Reduce Premature Deaths   59
12. Illicit Financial Flows: Dirty Development Money   63

13. Infant Mortality And Maternal Health: How To Save
    More Than 14 Million Newborns By 2030   66
14. Infectious Diseases: Ebola Kills Fewer Than Aids, TB
    And Malaria. What Should We Prioritize?   70
15. Infrastructure: The Digital Road From Poverty   74
16. Non-Communicable Diseases: Strokes, Heart Attacks
    And Cancer: Save 5M Lives Each Year   78
17. Nutrition: Feeding People Is Smart   82
18. Population And Demography: The Population Challenge   85
19. Poverty: Smart Ways To Tackle Poverty   89
20. Science And Technology: How To Make
    The World's Poor $500 Billion Richer   93
21. Trade: Why Embracing Freer Trade Could Be
    Our Best Chance To Help The World's Poor   97
22. Water And Sanitation: Investments In Water In Poor Nations
    Give Big Benefits   101

THE NOBEL LAUREATES' GUIDE TO THE SMARTEST TARGETS FOR THE WORLD   105

Smart Development Goals   109

Youth Forums   113

APPENDIX   117

The UN's 169 targets evaluated   119

The Open Working Group's Proposal
    for Sustainable Development Goals   121

Suggested further reading on Post-2015 Consensus   143

Authors of Post-2015 Consensus Assessment, Perspective and Viewpoint Papers

The authors who have contributed to the research for the Post-2015 Consensus are listed here. They are some of the leading academics and economists in their fields, together with a range of NGOs, UN Agencies, think-tanks and businesses. Together they provide a comprehensive assessment of the Post-2015 targets:

Air Pollution
Bjorn Larsen, Economist and consultant to international and bilateral development agencies; Marc Jeuland, Duke University; Mike Holland, Independent Consultant; Katharina M. K. Stepping, German Development Institute; Glynda Batham, Clean Air Asia

Biodiversity
Anil Markandya, Resource Economist; Alistair McVittie, Scotland's Rural College; Luke Brander, VU University Amsterdam and Hong Kong University of Science and Technology; Dilys Roe, IIED; Simon Milledge, IIED

Climate Change
Isabel Galiana, McGill University; Carolyn Fischer, Resources for the Future; Robert Mendelsohn, Yale University; ForumCC; Lucy Scott, Overseas Development Institute

Conflict and Violence
Anke Hoeffler, University of Oxford; James Fearon, Stanford University; S. Brock Blomberg, Claremont McKenna College; Rodrigo R. Soares, Sao Paulo School of Economics; Abigail E. Ruane, Women's International League for Peace and Freedom; Ciara Aucoin, Social Science Research Council; Olivia Russell, International Journal of Security and Development; Charles Ransford, Director of Science and Policy. Cure Violence

Data for Development
Morten Jerven, Simon Fraser University, Vancouver Canada; Gabriel Demombynes, World Bank; Justin Sandefur, Center for Global Development; Deborah Johnston, School of Oriental and African Studies, University of London; Serge Kapto, UNDP; Claire Melamed, Overseas Development Institute

Education
George Psacharopoulos, Member of CESifo Research Group; Paul Glewwe, University of Minnesota; Caroline Krafft, University of Minnesota; Peter Orazem, Iowa State University; Education International; Save the Children

Energy
Isabel Galiana, McGill University; Amy Sopinka, Advisor to the energy industry; Adele C. Morris, Brookings Institution; Todd Moss, Center for Global Development; Madeleine Gleave, Center for Global Development; Innovation: Africa; Lungile Mashele, Development Bank of South Africa

Food Security
Mark Rosegrant, International Food Policy Research Institute (IFPRI); Eduardo Magalhaes, International Food Policy Research Institute; Rowena A. Valmonte-Santos, International Food Policy Research Institute; Daniel Mason-D'Croz, International Food Policy Research Institute; Christopher B. Barrett, Cornell University; Boubaker BenBelhassen, UN Food and Agriculture Organization

Gender Equality
Irma Clots-Figueras, Universidad Carlos III de Madrid; Joyce P. Jacobsen, Wesleyan University; Elissa Braunstein, Colorado State University; Lindsey Jones, ACDI/VOCA; Anja Taarup Nordlund, Nordic Consulting Group Sweden; Almas Jiwani, UN Women National Committee Canada

Governance and Institutions
Mary E. Hilderbrand, George H. W. Bush School of Government and Public Service at Texas A&M; Aart Kraay, World Bank; Matt Andrews, Harvard Kennedy School; Martin Edwards, Seton Hall University; Nicola Crosta, Epic Foundation

Health Systems
Prabhat Jha, University of Toronto; Ryan Hum, University of Toronto; Cindy

Gauvreau, Centre for Global Health Research, St. Michael's Hospital, Toronto; Keely Jordan. Health Policy Researcher; Eileen Natuzzi, M.D., San Diego State University; Priya Madina, GlaxoSmithKline; Jon Pender, GlaxoSmithKline; Simon Wright, Save the Children; Douglas Webb, UNDP; Ilona Kickbusch, Graduate Institute of International and Development Studies in Geneva

Illicit Financial Flows
Alex Cobham, Center for Global Development in Europe; Tom Cardamone, Global Financial Integrity; Dev Kar, Global Financial Integrity; Peter Reuter, University of Maryland; Angela Me, UNODC; Semkae Kilonzo, Policy Forum

Infant Mortality and Maternal Health
Dara Lee Luca, Harvard University; Elizabeth Mitgang, Harvard University; Alyssa Shiraishi Lubet, Harvard University; David E. Bloom, Harvard University; Johanne Helene Iversen, University of Bergen; Kristine Husøy Onarheim, University of Bergen; Klaus Prettner, Vienna University of Technology; Günther Fink, Harvard School of Public Health; Patrick Gerland, United National Population Division, DESA; Danzhen You, UNICEF; Ann Starrs, Guttmacher Institute

Infectious Diseases
Anna Vassall, London School of Hygiene and Tropical Medicine; Neha Raykar, Public Health Foundation of India; Ramanan Laxminarayan, Public Health Foundation of India; Pascal Geldsetzer, Harvard School of Public Health; Salal Humair, Harvard School of Public Health and Lahore University of Management Sciences; Till Bärnighausen, Harvard School of Public Health; Maria Wang, Health Access Initiative; Regina Osih, Clinton Health Access Initiative; Peter Ghys, Joint United Nations Programme on AIDS (UNAIDS); José-Antonia Izazola-Licea, Joint United Nations Programme on AIDS (UNAIDS)

Non-Communicable Diseases
Rachel Nuget, University of Washington

Nutrition
Susan Horton, University of Waterloo; John Hoddinott, Cornell University; Rebecca Spohrer, Global Alliance for Improved Nutrition (GAIN)

Infrastructure
Emmanuelle Auriol, Toulouse School of Economics; Pantelis Koutroumpis, Imperial College London; Alliance for Affordable Internet; Charles Cadwell, Urban Institute

Population and Demography
Hans-Peter Kohler, University of Pennsylvania; Jere Behrman, University of Pennsylvania; Oded Galor, Brown University; Gregory Casey, Brown University; David Canning, Harvard School of Public Health; Michael Herrmann, United Nations Population Fund (UNFPA)

Poverty
John Gibson, University of Waikato; Gaurav Datt, Monash University; Valerie Kozel, University of Wisconsin-Madison; Deborah S. Rogers, Initiative for Equality and Stanford University

Science and Technology
Keith E. Maskus, University of Colorado; Kamal Saggi, Vanderbilt University; Pamela J. Smith, University of Minnesota; Padmashree Gehl Sampath, UNCTAD; Manuel F. Montes, The South Centre

Trade
Kym Anderson, University of Adelaide; Bernard Hoekman, European University Institute; Patrick Low, Fung Global Institute; Vinaye Ancharaz, International Centre for Trade and Sustainable Development; Santiago Fernández de Córdoba, UNCTAD and University of Navarra; David Vanzetti. Australia National University

Water, and Sanitation
Guy Hutton, World Bank Water and Sanitation Program (WSP); Dale Whittington, University of North Carolina at Chapel Hill; Mary Ostrowski, American Chemistry Council; Allan Jones, International Chemical Regulation.

How to read this book

The world will spend $2.5 trillion on the next set of global targets, 2016–2030. Let's spend it well.

This book is a unique guide to what we can do to make the world a better place in the next 15 years. It asks 60 teams of the world's top economists: Which targets are best?

Covering all areas, from health to education, from sanitation to illicit finances, it sets out to show how much good a dollar spent on any target will do for people, planet and prosperity.

See how good all targets are in the quick overview on pages 20–21. You can read about the costs and benefits of proposals within each topic area from Air Pollution (p23) to Water and Sanitation (p101). To read much more, sample the 100+ academic papers on post2015consensus.com.

You can read what our Nobel Laureates found to be the very best 19 targets for the world from page 105. You can read about the findings from the Youth Forums from across the world from page 113. And finally, you can see what the economists think of the UN's current proposal with 169 targets starting on page 119.

Coral reef protection, for instance, will deliver $24 of goods (better fishing, better ecosystems and more tourism) for every dollar spent (p27). Pre-school in Sub-Saharan Africa: $33 per dollar (p43). Tuberculosis treatment: $43 (p60). Infant nutrition: $45 (p83). And contraception: $120 (p67, 87). Successfully concluding the Doha round of trade negotiations, meanwhile, will make the world $11 trillion richer by 2030, or about $2,000 per dollar spent to pay off Western farmers (p97). Smart targets could literally make the world trillions of dollars better off each year.

The book is intended as a resource for anyone interested in helping the world – policy makers, economists, researchers, students and NGOs. Let's spend our resources to do the most good for the world.

INTRODUCTION

SMARTER GOALS FOR THE UN

Right now, the United Nations is negotiating one of the world's potentially most powerful policy documents. Over the next 15 years, it will influence more than $2.5 trillion of development aid to help pull hundreds of millions out of poverty and hunger, to reduce violence and improve education – essentially make the world a better place. But much depends on this being done well.

The UN has had a lot of well-meaning targets, goals and declarations being overlooked or even ignored over the decades. You probably didn't know that 2015 is the UN year of soils[1] and the year of light-based technologies,[2] nor that this is the decade for action on road safety.[3] All well-intentioned, but not all equally important or efficient.

Take education. Universal education has been promised in at least 12 UN sponsored declarations from 1950 to 2000[4], often invoking language from promises made first in 1934.[5] In 1961, the Addis Ababa Plan for instance promised that in Africa by 1980 "primary education shall be universal, compulsory and free."[6] Unfortunately, in 1980, about half of all kids of primary school age in Africa were still not in school.[7]

However, at the turn of the century something remarkable happened, when the largest gathering of world leaders in history – 100 heads of state and 47 heads of government[8] – descended on

---

[1] http://bit.ly/1ywY9R0
[2] http://bit.ly/1CDxggG
[3] http://bit.ly/1EI17qB
[4] http://bit.ly/19qQuip
[5] http://bit.ly/17kydBU
[6] http://bit.ly/1Fm37IK
[7] http://bit.ly/1CDxqVo, 43% in 1989, for Sub-Saharan Africa in World Bank it is 53.4% adjusted net enrollment rate, primary (% of primary school age children), http://bit.ly/1kuKDHe
[8] http://bit.ly/1E0YodX

the UN Millennium Summit in New York in September 2000. As is customary, they made lots of promises ranging from the grandiose "just and lasting peace all over the world" to specifics like urging the passing of the Kyoto Protocol and arguing for better safety for UN personnel.[9] But they also made a number of very specific promises, which later ended up as the Millennium Development Goals.

These were unique because they were short, specific and obvious development targets everyone could relate to – and because they had a clear deadline of 2015. In short, world leaders had staked out real and verifiable promises.

In reality, the MDGs had been worked out by a small group of people around the Secretary General. The goals emerged almost fully formed in Kofi Annan's *Millennium Report* published in April 2000,[10] and while they were formally adopted by all countries in September, they were really first thrashed out in August 2001 in collaboration with the IMF, the World Bank and the OECD.[11] There was no long, public deliberation or strong participation from governments[12] and this was likely one of the primary reasons that the end result was a sweet, short 8 goals and 18 targets.[13]

Moreover, most of the MDG conversation more or less disregards 11 of these official targets, leaving a simple 7 promises, as listed in the table on page 6. This is entirely sensible. Promises such as "halve the proportion of people in poverty from 1990 to 2015" seems worthy of a global goal. This is less true when target 8C implores the world to "Address the special needs of landlocked developing countries and small island developing states (through the Program of Action for the Sustainable Development of Small Island Developing States and the outcome of the twenty-second special session of the General Assembly)." And the promise to "achieve full and productive employment and decent work for all, including women and young people" is well-intentioned but superfluous (which government would not strive towards higher employment?), impossible (a well-functioning

---

[9] http://bit.ly/INgnuW
[10] p77-78, http://bit.ly/1vB74kn
[11] http://bit.ly/1EjJyNN, p297
[12] http://bit.ly/1A1OiI5
[13] p11, http://bit.ly/19qQJdt

labor market needs some unemployment to facilitate job changes), and possibly counterproductive (job protection rules can lead to higher rates of youth unemployment and increase poverty[14]).

The progress on these 7 targets has been remarkable. On hunger, almost 24% of all people in the developing world were starving in 1990.[15] In 2012, 'only' 14.5% were starving, and if current trends continue, the world will reach 12.2% in 2015, just shy of the halving at 11.9%.

Likewise, the MDGs promised to cut by half the proportion of poor.[16] In 1990, 43% of the developing world lived below a dollar a day. In 2010, the proportion had already been more than halved at 20.6% – on current trends the proportion will drop below 15% by 2015, showing spectacular progress.

On the other hand, the eternal promise of 100%, universal education will not be fulfilled by 2015, either.[17] From an economist's point of view, this is not surprising – getting to 100% is almost impossible and certainly very, very expensive. That is why we should always be suspicious of promises of 100 or zero percent.

Yet, education is much improved. From completion rates in the high 70s throughout the 1990s, the developing world now gets almost 9 out of 10 students through primary school, and will hit 91% by 2015.

So, the world is definitely a much better place. Not just on these three measurements but on all the 7 MDG promises – girls are now very close to gender equality in schooling,[18] many more have access to clean water,[19] maternal, child and infant mortality have almost halved.[20] And these are not just abstract statistics – in 1990, 12 million children died before reaching their 5th birthday. Today, with slightly more children, less than 7 million die.[21] Each year, more than 5 million more kids survive.

[14] http://bit.ly/1DB1o0a
[15] http://bit.ly/1AyCtLL, MDG 1.9 Undernourishment
[16] http://bit.ly/1AyCtLL, MDG 1.1 Poverty
[17] http://bit.ly/1AyCtLL, MDG 2.1 Primary completion
[18] http://bit.ly/1AyCtLL, Gender
[19] http://bit.ly/1AyCtLL, water
[20] http://bit.ly/1AyCtLL, respective targets
[21] http://bit.ly/1DkF7oA, with birth numbers from http://bit.ly/1L5BL8o

Of course, some of the improvement would likely have happened anyway. Access to clean drinking water has been slowly and steadily increasing, with no apparent difference around the time of the Millennium Summit. On this account, the MDGs probably deserve no extra credit.

And while poverty reduction has actually gained speed since 2000, this is to a large extent due to China's furious economic growth, which is unlikely to have been inspired by the UN declaration.

However, analysis shows that education and child and maternal mortality have likely sped up after 2000, and credit is at least partly due to the UN goals.[22] Also the enthusiasm stemming from the MDGs helped recover OECD development aid from a slump in the 1990s and saw a two-third increase from $82 billion in 2000 to $135 billion in 2013 (both in 2012 dollars).[23]

In short, the MDGs fired up the global imagination: With just 7 simple targets, the world promised to help our poorest, and although we didn't meet all goals, they helped push us to a much, much better place.[24]

Goal	Promise by 2015	Improvement?	Faster progress?	On Track?
Poverty	Halve the proportion of poor	Y	Y	Y
Hunger	Halve the proportion hungry	Y	N	N
Education	Full course of primary schooling	Y	Y	N
Gender	Gender equality in school	Y	N	Y
Child mortality	Reduce under-5 mortality by 2/3rds	Y	Y	N
Maternal mortality	Reduce maternal death by 3/4ths	Y	Y	N
Environment	Halve the proportion without clean drinking water	Y	N	Y

[22] http://bit.ly/1vRHTQ4: "The causal chain from international agreement to policy change to development outcomes is a long one with many confounding influences. Given that, it is impossible to say with any certainty what was the impact of the MDGs. Having said that, the evidence available fits a story which suggests that the MDGs may well have played a role in increasing aid flows in the new Millennium, and that aid may have had some role in improving outcomes."

[23] http://bit.ly/1mRGp2h, http://bit.ly/1L5C96O

[24] See http://bit.ly/MqIH8i. The figure strips away much of the technicalities (there are 18 actual promises, some of which have fallen by the wayside), and not all evaluations, though based on academic research, will agree on all estimates. From http://bit.ly/17kzB7r, again derived from http://bit.ly/17kzEA8)

What next after the Millennium Development Goals?

So what is next? Many, like Bill Gates, argue that we should continue to focus on these simple, sharp goals – an MDG II. After all, there are still far too many poor, hungry and dead, and the solutions are often cheap and simple. We can easily avoid malaria deaths (ensure access to mosquito nets and artemisinin treatment) and starvation (promote better yielding varieties, more fertilizer, less food diverted to biofuels).

But there are also obvious gaps in the MDGs. There is no discussion of the world's biggest environmental challenge: indoor air pollution, which causes one out of every 13 deaths globally. This is caused by almost 3 billion people cooking and keeping warm burning twigs and dung. The solution is to increase access to electricity to power a stove and a heater. More electricity will also boost productivity in agriculture and industry and pull millions out of poverty, as we have seen in China.

Likewise, the MDGs skirt the question of more free trade, although free trade is possibly the most important factor in pulling hundreds of millions out of poverty. World Bank models indicate that even a moderately successful Doha round (which we didn't get) could do amazing good. By 2020, such an agreement could add about $5 trillion to global GDP, with $3 trillion going to the developing world.[25] This would add about 10% annually to the third world GDP. Toward the end of the century, such a free trade agreement would likely lead to an increase in annual GDP of more than $100 trillion annually. Most would go to the developing world, adding about 20% to their annual GDP. In comparison, the total costs, mostly to wean developed-world farmers from subsidies, are more than 10,000 times smaller, at approximately $50 billion per year for a decade or two.

The UN has initiated a process to look at a new set of goals from 2016-2030, possibly called Sustainable Development Goals. Unlike the previous few goals that were set by a small group around Kofi Annan, the current process is a long, inclusive process.[26] One working stream, called the Open Working Group, comes from the Rio+20

---

[25] http://bit.ly/1DD465R
[26] http://bit.ly/1gfeJfn

environment conference, has had 23 meetings over two years among more than 90 nations, often for a week at a time.[27] Another comes from the development community, through a UN System Task Team and a high-level panel co-chaired by the Presidents of Indonesia and Liberia and the Prime Minister of the United Kingdom. Yet more come from national, global, regional and thematic consultations, an independent research network called Sustainable Development Solutions Network led by Jeff Sachs, and views from businesses through the UN Global Compact.

This is a recipe for lots of targets. Not surprisingly, one online tracker shows that there are now more than 1,400 targets proposed.[28]

But this deluge of targets is not a surprise: If the SDGs are successful, they could end up determining a large part of the period's $2.5 trillion development aid. Of course, everyone wants *their* favorite topic on the books.

Leading up to the UN General Assembly in September 2015 where the final list of targets will be set, countries, missions, UN organizations and NGOs will perform a complex dance to determine – and hopefully whittle down – the next set of targets.

The currently most prominent process, the Open Working Group, has gone from considering 139 targets to an almost impossible 212 targets to finally settle on a still baffling 169 wordy targets. These range from the ambitious (end tuberculosis and malaria by 2030) to the whimsical ("create incentives for sustainable tourism"), from the noble (universal education) to the impossible (achieve employment for all).[29]

Most in the UN system agree that few targets and even fewer goals is crucial for success. Yet, many seem to think about the process as if it was mostly about crafty wording – finding a clever way to distil 169 targets into a few, elegantly phrased goals that will reenergize the international system to tackle all the world's ills.

---

[27] http://bit.ly/1AgQcDF

[28] http://tracker.post2015.org/

[29] Charles Kenny describes the OWG 212 targets: "It wouldn't be right to describe this as a Christmas tree. It is perhaps closer to a plantation of Christmas trees." http://bit.ly/1nSPBF5

Likewise, it is often expressed in that targets should be "transformative", "universal" and "balanced." While well-meaning, such criteria are mostly spurious.

The dramatic reduction in poverty in the last 25 years is an unparalleled good, but it was incremental, not transformative. Even more importantly, it wasn't an outcome of deliberate, transformative policies. Likewise, a successful free trade agreement would be phenomenally positive but not transformational. Conversely, many intentionally transformational policies have more than a whiff of social engineering – the radical agrarian socialism in Cambodia in the late 1970s joins a host of similar historical examples that were definitely transformative but not desirable.

It is in vogue to demand that the next SDGs should be "universal", applicable to both developing and developed countries. While the sentiment is psychologically understandable, tackling malaria and lifting people above a dollar a day is simply not something that applies equally to poor and rich countries.

And when preference is given to targets that are "balanced," both addressing economic, social and environmental concerns, such apparent aesthetical symmetry may seem appealing, but it is likely to be a guide to bad targets. Trade tackles poverty, artemisinin drugs tackle malaria and emission targets tackle air pollution. We shouldn't intentionally try to make every target work on every ill.

The uncomfortable reality is that most targets and many goals ought to go. Look at the MDGs – they were a success exactly because we didn't promise to deal with everything, but promised just 7 simple and obvious targets.

Yet, any kind of pruning is incredibly hard, since all champions, be they organizations, nations or individuals, are simply pushing for their own favorite targets, from education to health, sustainable production and global warming.

The risk is that the targets that end up being chosen will be unduly skewed towards the ones with the best PR – the cutest animals, the scariest scenarios, the most touching pictures of crying babies.

We can do better.

What this book is about

The Copenhagen Consensus and the Australia Consensus have engaged in a project to determine which targets will do *the most good per dollar spent*. 60 teams of international top economists have estimated the costs and benefits of 107 top targets, taking into account not just the economic, but also health, social and environmental benefits to the world. UN agencies, NGOs and businesses in both South and North have contributed to the findings. An expert panel including several Nobel Laureates has evaluated the economic evidence to classify the targets from phenomenal to poor. And Youth Forums from around the global South are picking *their* best targets.

The Open Working Group 169 target proposal

Imagine taking the UN document and overlaying it graphically with economic evidence. Highlight the very best targets with dark green – the targets that will cost little but do more than 15 times as much economic, social and environmental good. Color the targets that will do between 5 and 15 times as much good as they will cost light green. Paint the fair targets yellow – targets that still do more good than they cost. And color the poor targets red – the targets that will cost more than the good they provide for the world. Backed by thousands of pages of peer reviewed economic research, such simple traffic light markings could crucially help the world's busy decision makers focus on picking the most effective targets.

This is, indeed, what we did with the last Open Working Group document, as you can see from page 119. Here, together with 32 top economists we've gone through the 169 targets. It highlights 13 great, green targets and also warns the UN negotiators of 9 very poor red targets. The results are sometime intuitive, sometimes provocative, but always revelatory in the polite UN context – pointing out that not all targets are equally good.

Look at target 3.3 on page 123. Reducing malaria and tuberculosis is a phenomenal target, painted dark green. Its costs are small because solutions are simple, cheap and well-documented. Its benefits are large, not only because it avoids death and prolonged, agonizing sickness, but also improves societal productivity and initiates a virtuous circle. Saving a life from malaria costs in the order of just $1000.

On the other hand, HIV eradication is both hard and much less effective – because of the higher costs and life-long treatment, it is only yellow, not green. Saving a life from HIV costs on the order of $10,000. Although it feels bad to even mention it, we can save perhaps 10 lives from malaria, for each life saved from HIV. Where should we spend our resources first?

Removing fossil fuel subsidies in third world countries is also dark green (see target 12.c on page 134). With generous state subsidies, gasoline is sometimes sold for a few cents per gallon, mostly to the benefit of middle- and high-income groups with cars. Reducing subsidies would stop wasting resources, send the right price signals, and reduce the strain on government budgets, while also reducing CO_2 emissions.

However, substantially increasing the share of renewable energy by 2030 (7.2 on page 128) sounds good but turns out to be bright red. It is an expensive way to cut just a little CO_2 and it gives power to fewer people, with less reliability. One study shows that $10 billion can lift 20 million out of darkness with renewables but 90 million out of darkness with gas.[30] Prioritizing renewable energy over access to energy leaves more than 3 out of 4 people in darkness.

Moreover, it ignores most of the problem of indoor air pollution from stoves, heaters and fridges. Instead, we should focus on getting more energy to poor people, which is a proven way to increase growth and reduce poverty.

Painting targets in red throughout the document was uncomfortable for the promoters of these targets, but also a real eye-opener. As the US UN ambassador said: "I really don't like you putting one of my favorite targets in red – but we all truly need to hear economic evidence that challenges us."

Placing other targets in green was obviously welcomed and quickly turned into ammunition to keep or bolster these targets.

Of course, economics is not the only measure of what the global society should choose for its priorities for the next 15 years. But it provides a crucial part of the information.

---

[30] http://bit.ly/17Le493

Why we need costs and benefits

Imagine that you are sitting in a high-class restaurant with a delicious menu in front of you – but that there are no prices and sizes on the menu. If you order, you have no idea whether the veal will cost one dollar or a thousand, whether it will feed one or your entire party. Unless you have an exceptionally good expense account, you would probably be a bit hesitant to order.

What we try to do is to put prices and sizes on the vast menu of well-meaning targets suggested for the world. Naturally, costs and benefits are not the only important pieces of information – just because caviar is expensive and has moderate nutritional value, doesn't mean we can't pick it from the menu. But choosing it, we will now know that we'll have fewer resources left for desert.

Documenting costs and benefits are an important part of the necessary information for the world's choices, providing headwind to poor targets and tailwind to smart ones.

Costs and benefits for individual problems

There are many challenges that this world faces. We have taken our starting point from the challenges identified by the High-Level Panel co-chaired by the Presidents of Indonesia and Liberia and the Prime Minister of the United Kingdom. This lists problems from biodiversity and conflict, through energy and health to population and trade. You can see the entire list in the index, and it takes up the chapters from Air Pollution on page 23 to Water and Sanitation on page 101.

For each challenge we have engaged with 3 teams of international top economists (making 60 teams in all). Take Education, which starts on page 41.

Here economist George Psacharopoulos, formerly of the London School of Economics and the World Bank, has assembled the best estimates for a variety of different schooling targets for 2016–2030, which you can see in the table on page 43. The first target proposes to "increase the preschool enrollment ratio in Sub-Saharan Africa from the present 18% to 59% by 2030." While the cost will be substantial, the benefits will deliver $33 of social, economic and environmental benefits for each dollar spent.

Economists Paul Glewwe and Caroline Krafft, both from the University of Minnesota, as well as economist Peter Orazem from Iowa State University have written economic commentaries on the estimates from Dr. Psacharopoulos. Furthermore, Education International and Save the Children, two NGOs, have written commentaries with one broadly agreeing and one arguing that we need more than economic prioritization. UNICEF Education, one of the main educational UN bodies, has written a commentary on the arguments from the economists. All of these documents can help clarify the arguments of which targets work and which targets should be avoided for the next 15 years, and the more than 100 academic pages can be downloaded for free from our website post2015consensus.com.

For this book, however, we have reduced the discussion on the economics of education to a couple of pages and two tables, as you can see, starting on page 41. This inevitably means that you will have to access the full set of papers on the web to gain all the nuances, but hopefully it allows you to gain a wide overview. It lets you compare the preschool target effectiveness ($33 per dollar spent) with other education targets such as 100% primary education in Sub-Saharan Africa ($7) and 100% secondary education (at $4 per dollar spent).

It also makes it easier to compare education with other challenges such as energy or infectious diseases, both of which have more than a 100 academic pages of material on the web, but are here represented with their own quick overviews on pages 45–48 and 70–73. Here you can compare the efficiency of money spent on a specific education target with targets for energy and infectious diseases.

If you want the full overview, turn to the figure on pages 20–21, which shows the very simple overview of the benefits per dollar spent across all the evaluated targets (not all 107, because somewhat overlapping and very similar targets have been left out for the individual chapters).

Which targets should we chose?

If we go with all 169 targets in the Open Working Group outcome we will be spending money on many targets that will do little or moderate good. As a first approximation, let us suggest that we will spend an equal amount of money on all the 169 targets. If so, and with the evaluation from the 32 economists we can estimate the average benefit of the first billions of dollars spent.[31]

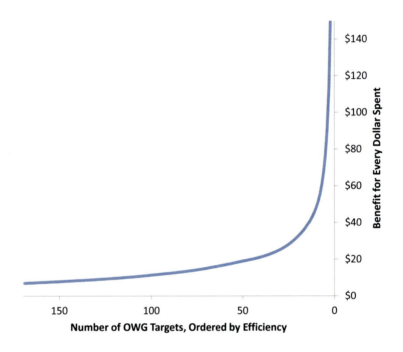

As you can see in the figure, if we pick all 169 targets, we will on average do $7 of good. This is not bad, but remember, it is an average of some very good spending and some very mediocre spending. With 169 targets we will be spending a small fraction on a few very, very good targets like contraception and free trade, and a large fraction on pretty poor targets. If we reduce the number of targets to the 100 best targets, the average benefit per dollar will rise to $12. This is because we have cut away some of the least effective targets. If we cut the number of targets to 50, we will be doing $19 of good for each dollar spent. If we pick just the 40 most effective targets, each dollar will do $21 of

---

[31] This becomes harder to estimate as we get fewer targets and as we spend more money, because some of the targets cannot appropriate all the spending. Also, we here estimate free trade efficiency very conservatively at $150, since the distribution would otherwise be very sensitively influenced by this one, very high number.

good. Picking just the 40 best targets means we will do *three times as much good for every dollar spent* compared to choosing all 169 targets ($21 versus just $7).

This shows us two things. Picking the low-hanging fruit or the very effective targets first will do much more good. But it also shows us that our intuition – that doing the most good means focusing on all good things – is simply wrong. If we want to help the world, it is not about making a long list of all the good things to do, but it is about focusing on the very, very best things to do first.

Promising everything to everyone gives us no direction. Having 169 priorities is like having none at all.

In bringing focus back to the world's targets, we should all take a page from Apple founder Steve Jobs:

> "People think focus means saying yes to the thing you've got to focus on. But that's not what it means at all. It means saying no to the hundred other good ideas that there are. You have to pick carefully. I'm actually as proud of the things we haven't done as the things I have done. Innovation is saying no to 1,000 things."[32]

How many targets we need to say no to is a political decision. Clearly we should not just make one or two promises to the world. But likewise, we should not make 169. I hope this book will help you make powerful arguments to influence your decision makers to pick the best 10, 15, 20 or 25 targets the world should focus on for 2030.

Our expert panel, including several Nobel Laureates, has reviewed all the research and has laid out its arguments for the 19 best targets for the world (page 105). Picking the 19 most efficient targets is equivalent to doing $32 of social good for every dollar spent – more than 4 times more efficient than the 169 targets.

Simultaneously, young people around the global South are giving their voice in a multitude of Youth Forums to show which targets they think should be picked. They typically pick 10–20 targets (page 113).

---

[32] http://bit.ly/1CDaSq7, Apple Worldwide Developer's Conference 13-16 May 1997.

It would have been great if the UN Secretary General Ban Ki-Moon had made his suggestions as to how to cut the number of targets significantly in his *Synthesis Report*. As Charles Kenny, senior fellow at the Center for Global Development in Washington, D.C., had suggested "The U.N. secretary-general has to edit down with an ax, not a scalpel." Unfortunately, his report was mostly a missed opportunity where the Secretary General made no real suggestions for edits.

Likewise, it would be great to see the countries themselves come up with a more concise list. However, with more than 90 governments having been involved in the process for more than two years, there is little interest in substantially revising the text.

Yet, we need to remember the UN has had lots of failed promises over the years, and one sparkling success: the short and sweet MDGs. Just like we know 18 targets work, we have a good reason to believe 169 targets will fail.

Showing which targets are great, good, fair and poor is an obvious step to making the next global targets smarter, but surprisingly that has never been done systematically before. And now you can read the economic evidence that clearly suggests which targets work and which don't.

Doing $35 trillion more good

If the world spends $2.5 trillion thinly spread over 169 targets, it will do $7 of good per dollar spent. In total, we will manage to do $15 trillion of extra good for the world. That is not to be scoffed at.

But if the same $2.5 trillion were spent more focused on the top 40 most efficient targets we could do $50 trillions of extra social, environmental and economic good for the world. Simply by focusing more on the best targets we could do an *extra $35 trillion of good* – equivalent to making everyone in the developing world an extra annual income.

Politics will still determine a large part of the final outcome, but I hope that you, together with the Nobel Laureates, the Youth Forums and the many, many academics involved in this project will help push for fewer, smarter targets.

Imagine if we could manage to change just *one* bad target to *one* phenomenal one.

Given that such a target will direct billions of dollars, and the phenomenal one can do $30+ more good for each dollar spent, we can end up helping the world to do hundreds of billions of dollars of more good. When leveraging the world's $2.5 trillion development budget, even the smallest difference to the world's next goals could be the best thing any of us gets to do this decade.

Post-2015 Targets

OVERVIEW OF TARGETS

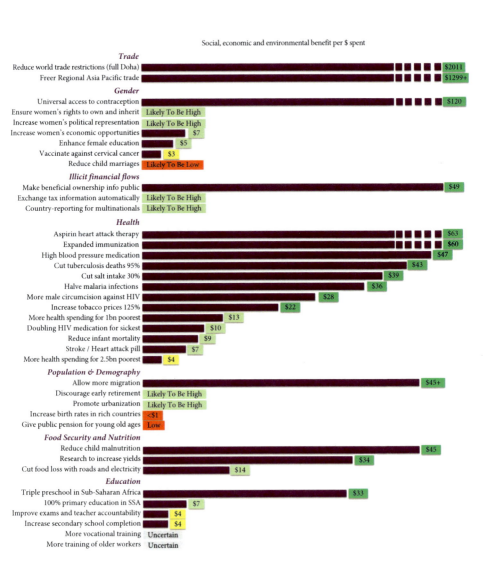

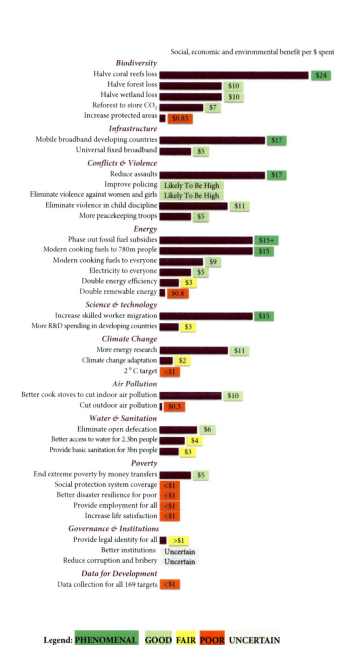

1. AIR POLLUTION
BETTER STOVES CAN REDUCE INDOOR AIR POLLUTION

Air quality has improved dramatically in rich countries over the past century. Around 1880, when the air was worst in London, it is estimated that 9,000 people died each year from air pollution,[1] about one of every seven deaths.[2] Today, London air is cleaner than since medieval times.

Yet, air pollution is still a huge problem, especially in the developing world. It kills 7 million people each year, or one of every eight deaths globally. This is not, however, the air pollution that most think about. The most deadly air pollution comes from *inside* people's houses, because 2.8 billion people still use firewood, dung and coal for cooking and keeping warm, breathing polluted air inside their homes every day.

To people, who don't live under these conditions, it is hard to imagine how dirty the indoor air is. The World Health Organization points out that the outdoor air in, for instance, Beijing, Delhi and Karachi is several times more polluted that the outdoor air in Berlin, London and Paris.[3] But the typical *indoor* air in a developing country dwelling with an open fire is many times more polluted than Beijing, Delhi or Karachi. That is why indoor air pollution kills 4.3 million people each year, making it one of the world's leading causes of death.

Yet, indoor air pollution is rarely among the big issues the world discusses. In 2000, the world made a number of smart, short promises for 2015 called the Millennium Development Goals, focusing on poverty, hunger, education and child mortality. These were mostly good promises, but indoor air pollution was missing.

---

1 http://www.sciencedirect.com/science/article/pii/S0921800911002953
2 (bit.ly/1AIYENC) estimates a death rate of nearly 300 per 100,000 or nearly 3 per thousand, compared to a little over 20 per thousand in total (bit.ly/1AIZ2Mh)
3 (bit.ly/1JmoJl6), Beijing PM10 is 121 in WHO overview (bit.ly/1CACMkc) and PM10 187 in (bit.ly/1vPtDav)

International Development Economist Bjorn Larsen has done a comprehensive study on air pollution and found both good – and less good – solutions.

The simplest solution is to replace inefficient, smoky stoves by more efficient, less smoky ones. Providing 1.4 billion people with such improved stoves would save almost 450,000 lives each year and avoid almost two and a half billion days of illness annually. Moreover, because the stoves are more efficient, they would on average save about 30% fuel, which translates into a savings of up to $57 per household per year, and at the same time make cooking more efficient providing valuable time savings. In total, the health and non-health benefits are estimated at about $52 billion per year. [Average of $74.6 and $29.8.]

What would it cost to make such a big improvement? In many parts of the world, an effective, improved stove costing just $30 is all that is needed to reduce indoor air pollution dramatically. The price is higher in some parts because of particular needs; in China, heating is needed as well as cooking, so the cost of an effective, improved stove rises to somewhat over a hundred dollars. Nevertheless, providing improved stoves for 50% of those cooking on unhealthy, smoky, traditional ones would cost about $5 billion per year.

So for every dollar spent on better stoves would do $10 worth of good. This gives us an excellent opportunity to compare this target for air pollution with all the other worthy targets proposed for the next 15 years.

However, helping 1.4 billion people with better stoves doesn't solve the problem. Another 1.4 billion are still cooking with unimproved stoves, and even improved stoves still cause more pollution than found in most cities. Moreover, some of the smoke from these improved stoves reaches outside so there is still pollution within the community.

A much cleaner solution is to get everyone to use gas. This would save 2.3 million deaths each year and avoid 13 billion days of illness, leading to more than twice the benefits. But unfortunately, gas stoves are more expensive and gas can cost about two hundred dollars each year per household, [using $40-50 per person in 4-5 person household.] so the costs are more than ten-fold higher. Even so, for every dollar spent, we would do two dollars of benefits, a respectable, but not nearly as good target. However, as the developing world gets richer a move to gas and eventually electricity will be both affordable and have obvious health benefits.

Reducing outdoor air pollution turns out to be much more costly. Better cook stoves and a transition to gas and electricity is an effective use of money that will also help reduce outdoor air pollution. But trying to reduce outdoor pollution with low-sulphur diesel or with filters on cars generally turn out to be too expensive. While benefits could reach $130 billion annually, the costs could exceed $300 billion per year.

Air pollution is one of the world's biggest and often overlooked challenges. And now we know that one of the best targets for the next 15 years is to get better stoves to 1.4 billion people, saving almost half a million lives each year.

Target	Cost $B p.a.	Benefit $B p.a.	Benefit for Every $ Spent
50% of those using unimproved cookstoves switch to improved cookstoves	5	52	$10
50% of those using unimproved cookstoves switch to LPG cookstoves	68	126	$2
100% of those using unimproved cookstoves switch to LPG cookstoves	137	297	$2
Outdoor particulate matter 2.5 does not exceed 35 μg/m3	50	13	$0.3
Outdoor particulate matter 2.5 does not exceed 25 μg/m3	98	35	$0.4
Outdoor particulate matter 2.5 does not exceed 15 μg/m3	190	78	$0.4
Outdoor particulate matter 2.5 does not exceed 10 μg/m3	304	130	$0.4

AIR POLLUTION DEATHS

	1990	2010	% of all deaths
Brazil	48 724	28 932	2%
Chile	5 480	2 734	3%
Colombia	11 696	9 085	3%
Costa Rica	713	585	3%
Ecuador	2 809	868	1%
Guatemala	7 089	6 575	8%
Mexico	33 269	35 807	6%
Peru	14 229	8 415	5%
Ethiopia	77 564	56 344	8%
Ghana	13 775	18 483	8%
Kenya	18 973	16 400	5%
Mali	14 663	14 195	7%
Mozambique	17 462	13 165	4%
Nigeria	109 185	99 757	4%
Rwanda	10 498	6 995	8%
South Africa	18 587	10 831	2%
Tanzania	27 097	20 960	5%
Uganda	20 976	15 149	4%
Zambia	8 890	8 989	6%
Egypt	46 415	53 208	10%
Iran	30 650	34 174	9%
Turkey	53 783	34 772	8%
Bangladesh	108 937	114 294	13%
China	2 571 772	2 273 250	23%
India	1 513 675	1 649 556	17%
Indonesia	196 880	228 477	15%
Nepal	31 324	28 895	16%
Pakistan	160 868	190 649	15%
Philippines	45 078	56 436	10%
Thailand	43 157	48 947	9%
Vietnam	79 195	76 268	15%

1990 & 2010 data from Global Burden of Disease Study and UNICEF

2. BIODIVERSITY
WHAT'S WORTH SAVING?

Biodiversity – the range of species we share our planet with – is important, but can we put a value on it? And can we estimate the benefits and costs of conservation? Professor Anil Markandya and two other economists (Luke Brander and Alistair McVittie) have written three new, scientific papers for my think tank, the Copenhagen Consensus. They find that not only can we estimate the costs and benefits for some projects but also that conservation can be a great investment.

A target to prevent the loss of coral reefs will for each dollar spent deliver at least $24 of environmental benefits. Likewise, the researchers find that reducing future loss of forests by half would likely do about $10 of good for each dollar spent. The economists also find that increasing protected areas is likely to be a poor target.

Of course, some of the obvious issues relate to adequate food, clean water and better schooling and healthcare. But humans don't live separately from the natural world. Rather, we rely on it for many different benefits or what experts call 'ecosystem services'. For example, forests don't just provide timber and firewood, but also provide flood protection, because they can soak up intense rainfalls – for instance, a big part of the reason Pakistan had such hugely damaging floods in 2010 was because large parts of its upper forests had been cut down. Here forests could have protected many of the poor that now saw their homes flooded or even their kids perish.

Forests also provide beauty experiences for residents nearby, while drawing in tourism, generating more benefits. At the same time, growing forests take up carbon dioxide from the air and lock it away for decades or even centuries while producing oxygen. And forests also provide refuge for enormous numbers of bird, animal and plant species, especially found in tropical rainforests.

All of these benefits can be valued. Timber has a commercial price, so that is straightforward. Locking away carbon can be priced based on likely costs of avoided climate damage, and likewise flood protection value shows up as reduced future floods. There is also a value for recreation and tourism, but not all of this is paid for by the users. Moreover, preserving species clearly have a benefit, but typically not one we pay for. This is where putting a price on a natural resources becomes more difficult, and economists have to fall back on surveys which ask people how much they are willing to pay to keep forests in place.

That makes it more difficult to put a firm value on a hectare of forest, but the academics all agree that spending a dollar is likely to do more than a dollar worth of good. The most likely outcome of a series of cost-benefit analyses show that setting the goal "reduce global forest loss by 50%" is likely to do about $5-$15 worth of social good for every dollar spent.

The same kind of analysis shows that preserving wetlands could be a good deal. The economists show that reducing global wetland loss by 50% will very likely do more good than its cost and most likely fall in the same range of about $10 back on each dollar.

More spectacular is the analysis for coral reefs, which both act as fishery hatcheries and fishing resources while storing abundant numbers of species. At the same time, coral reefs possess an amazing beauty, which both shows up in large tourism revenues but also in most individuals saying they are willing to pay a certain amount to make sure they continue to exist for our grand children. The analyses show that reducing global coral loss by 50% may cost about $3 billion per year but the total benefits likely run to at least $72, or about $24 back for every dollar invested.

However, economics also reveals poor targets: focusing to substantially increase protected areas is likely to cost so much – close to a trillion dollars – that it will generate less environmental benefit than the cost.

Of course, as we look to the next fifteen years, we have to spend most of our focus on the obvious wrongs with billions of people that are poor, lack food, water, health and education. But these analyses suggest that carefully crafted, environmental targets should also be a part of this solution.

Our job is to make sure that economic arguments are heard so we pick the smart targets but drop the poor ones, to make sure the next fifteen years help the world and its inhabitants as much as possible.

Biodiversity Targets	Benefit per $1 Spent
By 2030, stem the loss of coral reefs by 50%	$24
Reduce global forest loss by at least 50%	$10
Reduce wetlands losses by 50%	$10
By 2020, ecosystem resilience and the contribution of biodiversity to carbon stocks has been enhanced, through conservation and restoration, including restoration of at least 15 per cent of degraded ecosystems, thereby contributing to climate change mitigation and adaptation and to combating desertification.	$7
By 2020, at least 17 per cent of terrestrial and inland water areas and 10 per cent of coastal and marine areas, especially areas of particular importance for biodiversity and ecosystem services are conserved through effectively and equitably managed, ecologically representative and well-connected systems of protected areas and other effective area–based conservation measures and integrated into the wider lands.	$0.85

Share of total land area

	Covered by forest	Protected area
Brazil	62%	26%
Chile	22%	19%
Colombia	54%	21%
Costa Rica	52%	27%
Ecuador	38%	24%
Guatemala	33%	31%
Mexico	33%	13%
Peru	53%	19%
Ethiopia	12%	18%
Ghana	21%	15%
Kenya	6%	12%
Mali	10%	6%
Mozambique	49%	18%
Nigeria	9%	14%
Rwanda	18%	11%
South Africa	8%	6%
Tanzania	37%	32%
Uganda	14%	11%
Zambia	66%	38%
Egypt	0%	11%
Iran	7%	7%
Turkey	15%	2%
Bangladesh	11%	5%
China	23%	17%
India	23%	5%
Indonesia	51%	15%
Nepal	25%	16%
Pakistan	2%	11%
Philippines	26%	11%
Thailand	37%	19%
Vietnam	45%	6%

2012 data from The World Bank

3. CLIMATE CHANGE
IT'S TIME TO GIVE UP THE
TWO DEGREE TARGET

Climate change is certainly one of the most highly profiled issues of the 21st century so far. The UN Secretary-General argues that it is "an existential challenge for the whole human race."[1] On the other hand, when five million people were asked by the UN what they saw as most important, climate change came at the bottom of the list of 16 issues: way below healthcare, education, corruption, nutrition and water – and even below phone and internet access.[2]

This is astonishing, particularly given the consensus that climate change is real and happening. Are people right to be skeptical about current policies?

Economist Isabel Galiana has written the main paper on climate change and comes to a conclusion which is sure to be controversial: that present policies designed to reduce emissions of greenhouse gases are failing and cannot be effective until better technology is available. Despite the Kyoto Protocol and many national initiatives, the fact is that emissions have increased by almost half since 1990 and will continue to increase for many decades to come.

In stark contrast, the UN and many national governments focus on committing to keep the average temperature rise below 2°C above pre-industrial times. But there is a big problem: there is no realistic chance of keeping to this limit with current trends in fossil fuel use. To do this, emissions would have to peak and then be drastically cut with some technology capturing CO_2, liquefying it and injecting it deep underground. But this technology on the vast scale needed doesn't exist yet. Moreover, solar and wind, though very popular, will even in 2035 contribute just a tiny fraction of global energy needs.

The upshot is that pursuing this 2°C target is very costly and not guaranteed to be successful. Estimating all the economic, social and en-

[1] http://www.un.org/sg/statements/index.asp?nid=6482
[2] http://data.myworld2015.org/

vironmental costs and benefits are difficult, but one thing is clear: the program would cost much more than the benefits it would bring. In the meantime, that money could have been used to improve people's welfare in much more cost-effective programs.

Galiana suggests that investing 0.5% of global GDP into development of better energy technology would be a much better use of money. This could be funded with a slowly rising carbon tax (giving businesses an incentive to cut emissions but not telling them how to do it) and could give a payback of $11 for every dollar spent.

Galiana also suggests the world should spend 0.05% of GDP for adaptation, essentially helping many nations to cope better with specific climate impacts. Every dollar spent will likely do more than two dollars of social good.

Another economist who has contributed his perspective, Robert Mendelsohn, points out that the cost of action on climate change rises rapidly as the targets get tougher. Keeping average temperature rises below 5°C might cost about $10 trillion, but aiming for a 2° target would cost ten times as much.

Much better, then, to target a maximum of, say, 3°C rise, which will cost about $40 trillion but avoid most damages. If we insist on 2°C, we will pay an extra $60,000 billion dollars, but only prevent a stream of $100 billion damages that begins in 70-80 years. Moreover, all of these estimates assume cost-effective climate policies, whereas in real life they have often become many times more expensive.

Climate change is a big issue and cannot be ignored. But we need to take the emotion away and look at the facts; otherwise it will be the world's poorest that will suffer. Money which is not spent on costly, ineffective CO_2 cuts can be used to fund programs which are guaranteed to improve their lives.

Climate Change Targets	Benefit for Every Dollar Spent
Invest 0.5% of GDP in energy technology RD&D	$11
Invest 0.05% of GDP in adaptation	>$1 but region specific
Global annual carbon emission reduction targets for 2°C reduction, 450ppm	<$1
Emission intensity targets	Uncertain

Proposed Energy R&D spending

	million US$
Brazil	11 228
Chile	1 386
Colombia	1 892
Costa Rica	248
Ecuador	472
Guatemala	269
Mexico	6 305
Peru	1 012
Ethiopia	238
Ghana	241
Kenya	276
Mali	55
Mozambique	78
Nigeria	2 609
Rwanda	38
South Africa	1 753
Tanzania	166
Uganda	107
Zambia	134
Egypt	1 360
Iran	1 845
Turkey	4 111
Bangladesh	750
China	46 201
India	9 384
Indonesia	4 342
Nepal	96
Pakistan	1 161
Philippines	1 360
Thailand	1 936
Vietnam	857

2013 data from The World Bank

4. CONFLICT AND VIOLENCE
THE ECONOMICS OF VIOLENCE

Civil wars continue to rumble on in too many places: think Syria and a swathe of sub-Saharan Africa. Their consequences are devastating for those involved and they can blight a country's economic growth for years after they end. They make the headlines and are often a focus of international peace-keeping efforts via the UN and other agencies.

It is maybe somewhat counterintuitive, then, to argue that other forms of violence are actually a greater problem and deserve more of the world's attention, but this is exactly the case made by James Fearon and Anke Hoeffler in a paper for the Copenhagen Consensus project which will, we hope, make a useful contribution to the setting of post-2015 Sustainable Development Goals.

Take the stark fact that, for each civil war battlefield death, roughly nine people are killed in interpersonal disputes. 7% of these are children: more than one for every two civil war combatant killed. Think also that, almost by definition, it is difficult to arrive at a settlement to a civil war which all sides find acceptable. Interventions cannot be standardized, and the chances of long-term success are not always good.

If we consider the various categories of interpersonal violence, on the other hand, there are clear signs that things can and do improve. Falling homicide rates in high-income countries in general are a hopeful sign that continued economic development will create greater stability and reduce violence.

But there are also promising examples from middle-income countries where violence has otherwise become endemic. The homicide rate in Bogota in 1993 was 80 per 100,000 (eight times the level the WHO regards as an epidemic). The city followed a public health approach to the problem, trying to reduce the number of murders by using a range of measures including limiting hours of alcohol sales, disarmament and improvements to policing and the criminal justice system.

By 2004, the homicide rate had fallen to 21 per 100,000, still high but below Rio de Janeiro and Washington DC. If murder rates continued to fall at just half the average rate seen in the rich world and cities like Bogota, there would be 21% fewer deaths by 2030. With the estimated welfare cost of homicides alone equivalent to 1.7% of global GDP (six times the cost of civil wars) this makes a real difference.

A bigger issue still for the authors is the amount of violence against women and children. Child abuse covers a range of issues, but physical punishment alone is believed to have a welfare cost equivalent to 4.2% of global GDP, a staggering $3.6 trillion or the same as the total GDP of Germany.

Violence against women is mainly perpetrated by family members and includes beatings, forced marriage, rape and sexual assault and FGM and adds further to this total: assaults alone have an estimated cost of 5.2% of global GDP.

The current UN proposal is for a goal of eliminating violence against women and children by 2030, but this is purely aspirational. There is a danger with such unachievable goals of the best being the enemy of the good, and this paper proposes a more realistic target of halving the incidence of violence against women by their partners.

For other categories, targets include a reduction of 43% in the deaths of newborn babies (which is the stage at which the largest number of children are killed), and a range of interventions to reduce the very high level of homicides in many countries. As for the enduring problem of civil wars, Fearon and Hoeffler suggest that a 20% reduction in their number by 2030 is reasonable, given the past and present downward trend, but that specific effective international programs to prevent wars are unlikely to be possible.

The main purpose of the Copenhagen Consensus approach is to evaluate competing proposals on the basis of their costs and benefits, so that the international community can focus its finite resources on areas which will achieve the most good. No-one would argue that trying to reduce violence of all types is not a worthwhile goal, but this is an area where hard facts are difficult to come by.

A realistic figure for the economic cost of a homicide is something over $8 million. The overall costs of violence can be calculated using this and similar figures. The costs of some programs are also known, but most benefit-cost ratios are conjectural and, for many interventions, simply do not exist.

Other authors have contributed their own useful perspectives and viewpoints to this exercise. One clear theme is the need to conduct and measure the effects of various promising programs to see just where money can best be spent. Otherwise, targets may have to be far less ambitious, and focus on widespread problems which evidence shows are amenable to sensible actions, such as homicides.

Conflict and Violence Targets	*Benefit per $1 Spent*
Reduce assaults.	$17
Eliminate severe physical violence as a method of child discipline.	$11
By 2030, reduce the number of countries experiencing large scale wars (1000+ deaths) to 3 or fewer and the number of countries experiencing small scale wars (<1000 deaths) to 14.	$5
Improve policing.	Likely To Be High
Eliminate all forms of violence against women and girls.	Likely To Be High

Million US$ Yearly Cost of Violence

	Against Women	Against Children
Brazil	183 602	123 302
Chile	31 841	18 008
Colombia	37 364	30 159
Costa Rica	4 662	3 159
Ecuador	10 644	9 752
Guatemala	4 778	6 661
Mexico	153 200	126 671
Peru	23 402	20 314
Ethiopia	13 448	21 193
Ghana	7 441	9 493
Kenya	10 107	15 303
Mali	2 160	4 028
Mozambique	3 389	5 528
Nigeria	56 750	95 872
Rwanda	2 098	3 201
South Africa	90 740	81 823
Tanzania	9 715	16 225
Uganda	5 780	11 268
Zambia	2 963	5 333
Egypt	50 835	96 189
Iran	–	–
Turkey	68 653	61 539
Bangladesh	27 541	28 584
China	617 323	404 893
India	447 195	453 131
Indonesia	54 352	64 665
Nepal	3 793	4 649
Pakistan	43 655	55 041
Philippines	17 598	26 583
Thailand	34 657	21 797
Vietnam	16 892	14 103

2012 data from A Hoeffler & J Faeron and The World Bank

5. DATA FOR DEVELOPMENT
MEASURING THE NEXT GLOBAL DEVELOPMENT GOALS

Are we willing to pay $254 billion or almost two years of the next fifteen years of development aid, to get better data?

For the last decade and a half, the world has made a few, smart promises with the so-called Millennium Development Goals: half the proportion of hunger and poverty, get all kids in school and dramatically reduce child mortality. We have definitely seen a huge move towards success, although not all promises will be achieved.

But perhaps surprising, we have only little information about what exactly we achieved. While you can go on countless web-sites and see how well for instance Botswana is doing with poverty, the truth is that most of the data is based on just one household survey ... from 1993. Actually, most of the available numbers are not data but projections and estimates. In total, there are more gaps than real observations and the observations themselves are often dubious.

But we need to set aside resources to *measure* how well we tackle all these issues, and that has real costs. How much this will cost and how much the international community can justify spending in this way is the important topic covered by Professor Morten Jerven in his new paper for the Copenhagen Consensus.

Take the original MDGs. There were just 18 simple targets. Data collection for these targets was patchy, with many gaps, and much of the information collected was of dubious quality. However, Jerven collates the information we have about survey costs across the world and estimates that the proper monitoring of all 18 targets and 48 indicators would have cost the world $27 billion. That is a significant number, but given that the world will spend about $1.9 trillion over the period, it is a perhaps not unreasonable 1.4% to spend on getting information.

The problem is, that the next set of targets is growing ever larger. A high-level panel with PM David Cameron from the UK, President Yudhoyono from Indonesia and President Sirleaf from Liberia along with leaders from civil society and the private sector suggested 59 targets and advocated building "better data-collection systems, especially in developing countries."

And just a couple of months ago, 70 UN ambassadors in the so-called Open Working Group proposed a vertiginous 169 targets. One of these many targets argued that by 2020 the world should "increase significantly the availability of high-quality, timely and reliable data disaggregated by income, gender, age, race, ethnicity, migratory status, disability, geographic location and other characteristics relevant in national contexts."

Doing even a minimum data collection for all these 169 targets Jerven estimates will cost at least $254 billion, or almost twice the entire global annual development budget.

And this is a very low estimate, since it does not take account of basic administrative data gathering by national governments. Neither does it include costs for all the household surveys, which are recommended, since costs for these were impossible to obtain. And countries where data has not yet been collected, will likely prove even costlier. Remember, six of 49 countries in sub-Saharan Africa have never had a household survey and only 28 have had one in the last seven years.

Moreover, there is a serious question of capacity. Worldwide, only about 60 countries have the basic registration systems needed to monitor trends in social indicators. Many poor countries – the ones whose citizens have the most to gain from effective development programs – do not have the capacity to collect useful data on a national basis. In the $254 billion estimate there is no allowance for maintaining the statistical office, training and retaining personnel, analyzing along with disseminating the data. There is ample evidence that the MDG agenda has already stretched statistical capacity and strained statistical offices in poor countries and that 169 new targets will only make it much worse.

Most participants discussing the Sustainable Development Goals recognize that we need *much, much* fewer targets. And that is the process the Copenhagen Consensus tries to help inform by publishing how much targets will cost and how much environmental, social and economic good they will do.

So when informed of the formidable costs of data collecting for each target, it is reasonable to reconsider the best number of targets. One interesting point of comparison is looking at what industrialized countries spend on statistics. For example, both the Norwegian and British governments have official statistical services, which cost about 0.2% of GDP. Using this figure as a measure of willingness to pay would suggest that we should aim more at *four* SDG targets, which could be properly monitored, rather than an unwieldy 169.

Data for Development Target	Benefit for Every Dollar Spent
Enable the High Level Panel's data revolution for the OWG's 17 goals and 169 targets	Likely to be < $1

6. EDUCATION
THE TROUBLE WITH UNIVERSAL EDUCATION

Universal education is a noble goal which has proved impossible to achieve so far. Since 1961's UNESCO ambition of achieving 100% primary enrolment by 1980 (from a then baseline of 40%), a series of goals has been missed and simply reformulated with a later target date. The post-2015 proposals follow the trend by pushing targets forward to 2030, while 60 million children remain out of school.

Something isn't working, but the prescription is often just more of the same: more money to fix the problem but with too little consideration about how best to spend it. Abandoning the unachievable target of universal education may be difficult for idealists to accept, but first targeting those who can really benefit will be better for both individuals and society.

Rather than simply sticking to a failed utopian vision, it is time for the international community to prioritize targets and focus limited resources on the most cost-effective. This is the message in a paper by George Psacharopoulos, formerly of London School of Economics and the World Bank, the first in a series commissioned by the Copenhagen Consensus Center looking at the post-2015 development agenda.

Of course, even if more international aid was the right answer, there would be a strong argument in favor of doing a cost-benefit analysis of proposed programs. There are many competing views of how aid should be spent and, in the real world, only a selection can be properly supported.

And the problem is that if we look at just schooling and pre-schooling for all, we could easily end up spending way more than the *entire* global education budget. This is clearly not sustainable.

So, Psacharopoulos points out we need to look at what works best first; primary and pre-school education. When setting priorities, there are several reasons why it is best to focus on early years' education. Children are highly receptive to knowledge when young, there is generally no cultural barrier to education of girls and young children can contribute relatively little in terms of labor. In simple terms, starting early gives young children a head start for continued learning; it is also cheaper to deliver early years' education.

The immediate benefits of this are well established, but the longer term effects are both more profound and less obvious. The initial learning boost from attending pre-school does not provide an advantage for long compared to peers in primary school. However, this early intervention does give an unexpected payback later in life, with adults earning more. It seems that pre-schooling gives children a boost in social skills or emotional development which is not easy to quantify.

Although early education is the favored choice of many economists, estimating the return on investment is not an easy task. However, to make choices between different education targets and goals from other areas – health and nutrition, for example – estimates have to be made.

While it is straightforward enough to work out the costs of education – mainly the obvious costs of providing teachers and school buildings, plus the lost value of child labor – the benefits are less clear-cut. But based on the most extensive data collected, Psacharopoulos shows that the best target is likely to be: "Reducing by 50% the number of children who are not attending preschool in sub-Saharan Africa" which has a benefit-cost ratio of 28 to 39.

While this sounds like a rather modest target, it focuses resources where they can do most good and, unlike the failed goals of previous decades, is realistic and achievable. Sub-Saharan Africa is where the greatest problems lie and where the most can be achieved. Early years' education gives children a head start in life, improves their life-long earning power and has wider societal benefits not captured in the estimated benefit-cost ratio.

The more ambitious target of universal primary education has a benefit-cost ratio of 3-6, while focusing on achieving 100% primary education in SSA alone shows a benefit-cost ratio 6-8. The much lower returns compared with the 50% target in sub-Saharan Africa reflect the fact that marginal costs rise as the easier goals are reached first. Concentrating on the most cost-effective goal would be a better use of scarce resources.

Quality of education is also undeniably important, but hard to achieve. Extra expenditure on factors like reduced class sizes alone make surprisingly little impact, but investment in institutional changes to such things as exams and teacher accountability could give a BCR of 3-5. On the other hand, the jury is still out on vocational training, but often general secondary education is more profitable than vocational education, meaning it is a poor investment.

If the world's poorest are to be helped the most, tough choices have to be made between competing goals. In an ideal world, universal, high quality secondary education would be an excellent goal, but first the urgent problem of basic level education in the world's most deprived regions has to be addressed. This way, we have the best hope of doing the most good with limited resources over the next 15 years.

Education Targets	Benefit for Every Dollar
Increase the preschool enrollment ratio in Sub-Saharan Africa from the present 18% to 59%	$33
Increase the primary enrollment ratio in Sub-Saharan Africa from the present 75% to 100%	$7
Increase student test scores by one standard deviation	$4
Ensure secondary school completion	$4

Basic education indicators

	Primary school enrollment	Adult literacy
Brazil	–	91%
Chile	93%	99%
Colombia	86%	94%
Costa Rica	93%	97%
Ecuador	97%	93%
Guatemala	95%	78%
Mexico	98%	94%
Peru	96%	94%
Ethiopia	–	39%
Ghana	82%	71%
Kenya	83%	72%
Mali	73%	34%
Mozambique	86%	51%
Nigeria	66%	51%
Rwanda	99%	66%
South Africa	90%	94%
Tanzania	98%	68%
Uganda	91%	73%
Zambia	98%	61%
Egypt	97%	74%
Iran	100%	84%
Turkey	95%	95%
Bangladesh	96%	59%
China	100%	95%
India	99%	63%
Indonesia	95%	93%
Nepal	98%	57%
Pakistan	72%	55%
Philippines	89%	95%
Thailand	96%	96%
Vietnam	98%	94%

2009-2013 data from UNICEF

7. ENERGY
HOW INDOOR STOVES CAN HELP SOLVE GLOBAL POVERTY

Nutritious food, clean water and basic healthcare for all may look like obvious high-priority targets for the international community, but we shouldn't ignore energy. The use of wood and coal in steam engines kicked off the Industrial Revolution, which led to today's prosperous, modern societies. Reliable and affordable energy is just as vital for today's developing and emerging economies. Driven mostly by its fivefold increase in coal use, China's economy has grown 18-fold over the past thirty years while lifting 680 million people out of poverty.

The energy ladder is a way of visualizing stages of development. This starts with what we call traditional biofuels – firewood, dung and crop waste. Almost three billion people use these for cooking and heating indoors, which is so polluting, the World Health Organization estimates they kill one of every thirteen people that die on the planet.

The next step on the ladder is 'transition fuels' such as kerosene, charcoal and LPG. The top rung of the ladder is electricity, which thankfully makes no pollution inside your home. Because the electricity is often powered by fossil fuels it does contribute to the problem of global warming. Hence an alluring option could be to move to clean energy, like wind, solar and hydro. Some are suggesting that developing countries should skip the fossil step and move right to clean energy. However, rich countries are already finding the move away from coal and oil to be a difficult one, and there are no easy answers for developing economies.

So, what about the almost-three billion cooking with dirty open fires? Should they take higher priority than the broader, long term objective of cutting back on fossil fuel use? It turns out there are smart ways to help on both accounts, say Isabel Galiana and Amy Sopinka, the two economists who wrote the main paper on energy.

Burning firewood and dung on open indoor fires is inefficient and causes horrendous air pollution. More than four million people each year die from respiratory illness because of smoke from indoor open fires. Most of these are women and young children. Women and children are also the ones who have to spend their time fetching firewood, often from quite far away. Providing cleaner cooking facilities – efficient stoves which run on liquefied gas – would improve health, increase productivity, allow women to spend time earning money and free up children to go to school.

The economic benefits of getting everyone off using dung and wood are as high as the human welfare ones: more than $500 billion each year.[1] Costs would be much lower. Including grants and subsidies to purchase stoves, annual costs would run about $60 billion. Every dollar spent would buy almost nine dollars of benefits, which is a very good way to help.

However, the economists also provide a more realistic target, which turns out to be even more efficient. Since it is awfully hard to get to 100%, they suggest providing modern cooking fuels to 30%. This will still help 780 million people, but at the much lower cost of $11 billion annually. For every dollar spent, we would do more than $14 worth of good.

While clean cooking is important, electricity can bring different benefits. Lighting means that students can study after dark and family activities can continue into the evening. Clinics can refrigerate vaccines and other medicines. Water can be pumped from wells so that women do not have to walk miles to fetch it.

The value of getting electricity to everyone is about $380 billion annually. The cost is more difficult to work out. To provide electricity to everyone would need the equivalent of 250 more power stations, but many rural areas might best be served by solar panels and batteries. This is not an ideal solution, but would still be enough to make an enormous improvement to people's lives. The overall cost is probably around $75 billion per year. That still does $5 of benefits for each dollar spent.

If we want to tackle global warming, on the other hand, there are some targets we should be weary of, whereas others are phenomenal. One prominent target suggests doubling the world's share of renewables, particularly solar and wind, but this turns out to be a rather ineffective use of resources. The extra costs of coping with the intermittent

---

1 $536, median of $178.6-$893.

and unpredictable output of renewables makes them expensive, and the cost likely to be higher than the benefits.

However, the world spends $544 billion in fossil fuel subsidies, almost exclusively in third world countries. This drains public budgets from being able to provide health and education, while encouraging higher CO_2 emissions. Moreover, gasoline subsidies mostly help rich people, because they are the only ones who can afford a car. To phase out fossil fuel subsidies would be a phenomenal target, because it would cut CO_2 while saving money for other and better public uses. The economists estimate that every dollar in costs would do more than $15 of climate and public good.

With such high-return targets, the economic evidence shows that – if carefully chosen – energy targets should definitely be part of the promises for the next 15 years.

Energy Targets	Costs ($B) per year	Benefits ($B) per year	Benefit for Every Dollar Spent
Double Research, Development and Demonstration (RD&D) in Energy. Technologies			$16
Phasing out Fossil Fuel Energy Subsidies	<$45	$675	>$15
Provide Access to Modern Cooking Fuels to 30% of the Population	$11	$161	$15
Universal access to modern cooking facilities	$61	$536	$9
Universal energy access	$135	$916	$7
Universal electrification access	$74	$380	$5
Double the Rate of Energy Efficiency Improvement Globally	$213	$576	$3
Double the Share of Renewable Energy in the Global Energy Mix	$514	$415	$0.8

Electrification and Household Air Pollution

	People without electricity	Urban Electrification	Rural Electrification	Household air pollution deaths
Brazil	1 000 000	100%	97%	21 350
Chile	–	–	–	1 330
Colombia	1 400 000	100%	89%	7 502
Costa Rica	0	100%	98%	226
Ecuador	900 000	99%	84%	486
Guatemala	2 200 000	96%	75%	5 192
Mexico	–	–	–	15 311
Peru	2 700 000	99%	65%	6 420
Ethiopia	70 400 000	85%	10%	45 698
Ghana	7 100 000	90%	52%	13 399
Kenya	34 500 000	60%	7%	15 676
Mali	10 800 000	55%	12%	9 749
Mozambique	15 400 000	66%	27%	12 858
Nigeria	92 900 000	55%	35%	69 005
Rwanda	9 500 000	67%	5%	5 680
South Africa	7 700 000	88%	82%	7 623
Tanzania	36 300 000	71%	7%	20 353
Uganda	31 000 000	55%	7%	13 213
Zambia	10 400 000	45%	14%	8 629
Egypt	300 000	100%	99%	3 452
Iran	1 200 000	100%	95%	1 886
Turkey	–	–	–	6 647
Bangladesh	62 200 000	90%	48%	78 281
China	2 500 000	100%	100%	1 039 360
India	303 700 000	94%	67%	1 022 130
Indonesia	59 500 000	92%	59%	164 651
Nepal	6 500 000	97%	72%	19 534
Pakistan	56 100 000	88%	57%	114 806
Philippines	28 700 000	89%	52%	48 221
Thailand	700 000	100%	99%	24 520
Vietnam	3 500 000	100%	94%	45 502

2010 data from Global Burden of Disease Study & 2012 data from IEA

8. FOOD SECURITY
BUILD ROADS IN DEVELOPING WORLD TO BOLSTER FOOD SUPPLIES

Almost one-quarter of all food in the world is lost each year, from harvesting and storage to wastage in the consumer's kitchen.[1]

We can expect almost a doubling of demand for food until 2050.[2] This is both because the world will add another two billion mouths to feed, but also because of a surging new middle class will demand much more meat and dairy products, which again requires much more animal feed.

Fortunately, new analyses show that there are smart ways to reduce the world's enormous food waste. For every dollar spent we can end up doing $13 of good ensuring more food security for the world. Interestingly, these solutions have little to do with the food waste campaigns heard through most of the rich world.

So, what is the best way to increase food security? This is a really vital issue because, if people aren't properly fed, they get sick more easily and can't work well, while children's growth is stunted, disadvantaging them for the rest of their lives. Avoiding waste in the food chain – in the field, during processing and storage and in people's houses – seems like a really good way to make the most of the crops a farmer grows.

In the rich world, the focus is mostly on food waste with the consumer. This makes sense, because more than half is lost in first world kitchens. But this is also because we can afford it – in the UK, the most wastage comes from salads, vegetables and fruits[3], which are luxury goods compared to the cheapest calories like grains and tubers eaten throughout the poor world. Likewise, smaller households waste more per person, because it is harder to put everything to use, while richer

---

1 http://dx.doi.org/10.1016/j.scitotenv.2012.08.092
2 Barrett, footnote 4, 70-100% increase.
3 http://rstb.royalsocietypublishing.org/content/365/1554/3065

households waste more because they can afford the extra luxury of buying 'just to be safe'.

The world's poor lose little of their food, simply because they can't afford to. In Africa, food waste loses 500 calories per person every day – but just 5% are lost with the consumers.[4] Instead more than three-quarters are lost in agricultural production, both when birds and rats eat them during harvesting and when pests spoil them in storage.

There are many smart solutions – from simple curing of roots, tubers and bulbs, to expensive refrigeration. All of these technologies are very good investments in industrialized countries, so why aren't they adopted in the developing world? In a new report, a team of economists from the International Food Policy Research Institute pointed out the main problem is lack of infrastructure. Simply put, if there are no proper roads, farmers cannot easily sell their surplus produce, which may then spoil before it can be eaten. The researchers found that four key factors could make a real difference to losses in the food chain: an electricity supply, paved roads, rail capacity and road capacity. These mean that farm produce can be sent to market and other food supplies brought in, and that grains can be dried or vegetables kept cool.

They estimate the overall cost to approximately halve post-harvest losses in the developing world would cost $239 billion over the next 15 years, but it would generate benefits of just over $3,000 billion, generating $13 of economic benefits for every dollar spent.

This has real-world impacts – it will bring down food prices to make food more affordable for poor people. By 2050, better infrastructure could mean that 57 million people – more than the current population of South Africa – would no longer be at risk of hunger. In particular, about 4 million children would no longer suffer from malnutrition. Most of these gains would be in sub-Saharan Africa and South Asia, the world's most deprived regions.

But it turns out there is an even better food target. Per dollar spent, we can achieve thrice the economic benefits and larger reductions in the number of people at risk of hunger and the number of malnourished children by focusing on higher efficiency rather than on preventing food losses.

---

4 Table 4S, http://dx.doi.org/10.1016/j.scitotenv.2012.08.092

Today, only about $5 billion is spent each year on research to improve the seven major global food crops, and just 10% of that is targeted to help small farmers in Africa and Asia. Investing an extra $88 billion in agricultural research and development over the next 15 years will increase yields by an additional 0.4% each year. This would reduce prices and improve food security to give nearly $3 trillion worth of benefits, an enormous $34 of good for every dollar spent.

We all want to help get a better world by 2030. If we listen to the economic evidence and pick the best targets, we can make sure, resources are spent doing the most good possible. The new research makes a strong case for including targets on yield research and agricultural waste to our promises.

Targets		Benefits ($B)	Costs ($B)	Benefit for Every $ Spent
Reduce post harvest losses by 10 percentage points	Globally	$4,051	$299	$14
	Developing World	$3,072	$239	$13
Increase investment in agricultural R&D by 160%		$2,961	$88	$34

Food waste

	Calories wasted	Waste reduction could feed million people
Sub-Saharan Africa	21%	96
Europe	29%	133
Industrialized Asia	25%	254
Latin America	25%	96
North Africa & West Central Asia	26%	72
North America & Oceania	32%	117
South & Southeast Asia	18%	216
Global	24%	984

Data from M. Kummu et al 2012

9. GENDER EQUALITY
PUTTING GENDER EQUALITY ONTO THE POST 2015 DEVELOPMENT AGENDA

Even in today's rich societies, there is continued inequality between the sexes; women tend to be in lower-paying jobs, be less well represented in politics and the upper levels of business and bear the brunt of domestic violence. But the situation in parts of the developing world is much worse; traditional cultural norms mean that many girls receive little education, are married and bear children while still adolescents and cannot even open a bank account.

Gender equality is a big issue with a number of important components. Reproduction is one of them, and allowing women control over pregnancy means fewer deaths in childbirth, reduces infant deaths and gives mothers more time to devote to bringing up their family and earning an income. That's why putting money into family planning programs turns out to be such a good investment. But this is not the only way to think about gender equality. The best way to reduce violence against women, ensure they have equal rights and lift them out of poverty is to get out of the cycle of early marriage and childbirth, and empower them to be full members of society.

This is easier said than done, of course, but one good approach is to keep girls in school for longer and to make sure that well-paid jobs are available for them when they finish education. For example, in rural India, recruiters for well-paid back-office jobs for businesses visited randomly-selected villages over a period of three years. Those villages saw more female employment and women aged 15-21 were 5-6 percentage points less likely to get married or give birth over this period. Moreover, the better job opportunities gave an incentive to get better educated, with younger girls staying more in school and women enrolling in after-school training courses.

When we look at the evidence across a number of different studies and countries, each dollar spent on improving women's access to economic opportunities does $7 of good.

Improving female education is also a good target, but one that is notoriously difficult to achieve. In studies, it is shown that for each dollar spent, the benefits are likely to amount to about $5 of social good.

There are plenty of other possible targets which seem self-evidently a good thing, but for which we do not have estimates of costs or benefits. For example, ensuring women have equal rights to inherit, sign a contract, register a business or open a bank account would cost very little, but would have far-reaching benefits, but we simply do not have the data to quantify them.

Increasing women's political representation would also carry little cost, whereas the benefits would often be welcome but difficult to quantify. Essentially, the different priorities of women would begin to take equal precedence with those of men.

Female equality is a complex issue and is not going to be achieved using a set of neat, standardized solutions. However, economic analyses can help show where we can do the most good. Clearly, family planning can be one of the best targets we can put on the UN list of priorities, because it will do $120 of social good for each dollar spent. But many other ways, like education, economic opportunity, along with female rights and more equal opportunities vie for a place among the other priorities of nutrition, health and poverty.

Gender Equality Targets	*Benefit For Every Dollar Spent*
Improve access to sexual and reproductive health for all women.	$120
Improve women's access to economic opportunities.	$7
Increase the number of years of education attained by women.	$5
Ensure equal rights of women to own and inherit property, sign a contract, register a business and open a bank account.	Likely. To Be High
Increase women's political representation.	Likely. To Be High
Reduce violence against girls and women.	Unknown. but costs likely to be high, and effectiveness uncertain
Reduce child marriage.	Unknown. but costs likely to be high, and effectiveness uncertain

Gender equality

	Female legislators, senior officials and managers	Female professional and technical workers	Female members of parliament	Female wage of male wage for similar work
Brazil	37%	55%	8%	51%
Chile	24%	47%	16%	50%
Colombia	53%	54%	–	56%
Costa Rica	36%	44%	33%	62%
Ecuador	36%	50%	42%	–
Guatemala	45%	46%	13%	64%
Mexico	32%	45%	38%	54%
Peru	30%	43%	22%	54%
Ethiopia	26%	32%	28%	69%
Ghana	39%	34%	11%	59%
Kenya	–	–	19%	70%
Mali	–	–	10%	61%
Mozambique	–	–	39%	64%
Nigeria	–	–	7%	76%
Rwanda	34%	42%	64%	–
South Africa	30%	51%	45%	62%
Tanzania	17%	38%	36%	65%
Uganda	20%	42%	35%	73%
Zambia	19%	32%	11%	79%
Egypt	10%	37%	–	78%
Iran	15%	35%	3%	59%
Turkey	12%	37%	15%	62%
Bangladesh	6%	24%	20%	57%
China	17%	52%	24%	63%
India	–	–	12%	56%
Indonesia	21%	48%	17%	69%
Nepal	14%	19%	30%	62%
Pakistan	3%	22%	21%	55%
Philippines	48%	61%	28%	79%
Thailand	28%	56%	–	81%
Vietnam	23%	52%	24%	63%

2014 data from World Economic Forum

10. GOVERNANCE AND INSTITUTIONS
HOW CAN THE UN MEASURE IF BETTER GOVERNANCE PROGRAMS WORK?

Corruption last year cost the world more than one trillion dollars.[1] That is a trillion dollars we can't use to get better health care, education, food and environment. And corruption is only part of the problem of poor governance – many countries are run ineffectively, lacking accountability, transparency and rule of law.[2]

Running countries better would have obvious benefits. It would not only reduce corruption but governments would provide more services the public wants and at better quality. It is also likely that economic growth would increase. In a recent UN survey of seven million people around the world, an honest and responsive government was fourth in the list of people's priorities, with only education and healthcare and better jobs being rated higher.

But how should we get better governance? This is an important question as the world is considering what goals to set, especially given that the Millennium Development Goals didn't even mention governance. For the Post-2015 Agenda, targets for governance have been proposed, recognizing that if there is corruption, most of the money for food may go elsewhere, and if there is little institutional control, ambitious environmental rules may just be flouted.

Mary E. Hilderbrand of the Center for International Development at Harvard has written the main paper on improving governance. As she points out, it is obvious that well-governed nations are better than ill-governed ones. But there are two problems.

The first problem revolves around whether good governance is a prerequisite for development or a consequence of it. Historical analyses have shown that having good institutions such as security of property

---

[1] http://bit.ly/1CARkAq, this is better than the $2.6 trillion estimated here: http://www.oecd.org/cleangovbiz/49693613.pdf
[2] http://www.unescap.org/resources/what-good-governance

rights is the single most important factor behind the variation in wealth of countries, and that more corruption goes together with less economic growth. That seems to suggest that better secured property rights and less corruption will generate more wealth. However, further analyses have shown that it could just as easily be that higher wealth and economic growth lead to better governance. For now, it is hard to say that good governance is the main way to start a virtuous circle.

The second problem is that we don't know much about *how* to get good governance. A study of 80 countries where the World Bank had programs to improve governance showed that governance improved in 39% of countries but worsened in 25% – what could look like a moderate success. However, all the countries the World Bank *didn't* help had similar success and failure rates – suggesting that the World Bank programs had made no difference.

The simple point is that while everyone can agree it would be great to get rid of corruption and have more transparent and accountable government, we often know very little about how to achieve it. That is why proposed targets like "Substantially reduce corruption and bribery in all its forms" sound great, but are essentially well-meaning slogans with little content.

Indeed, Hilderbrand finds that many proposed targets are too generalized and some even a poor use of resources.

However, she does find one target that would do a lot of good for each dollar spent. "By 2030 provide legal identity for all, including birth registration." This may sound like a very unambitious step to those of us lucky enough to live in prosperous democracies where such things are taken for granted, but it would be a major step forward for many developing countries.

Importantly, this is a measurable outcome, so progress can be monitored. It also means that there must be functioning public services to provide registration facilities and maintain records. Building this capacity in a single well-defined area would provide a clear model for how other services can be provided effectively. It is also unlikely in any case that a registration service would exist in a vacuum; an effective one would almost certainly be a sign of an emerging public service competence.

There are also real benefits to each citizen of having a proper legal identity. It helps them to claim their legal rights, for example, and would certainly also help to establish property rights, which are vital to allow individuals to prosper and the economy to grow. Elections become less vulnerable to corruption when voters are properly registered. And, as an economy grows, a proper legal identity is essential for opening a bank account or getting a driving licence.

Good governance is important. But instead of platitudes we should focus on measurable, attainable targets that will actually make a big difference for the next 15 years.

Target	Benefit for every dollar spent
Provide legal identity for all, including registering all births	More than $1
Develop effective, accountable and transparent institutions at all levels	Uncertain
Ensure responsive, inclusive, participatory and representative decision-making at all levels	Uncertain
Ensure public access to information and protect fundamental freedoms, in accordance with national legislation and international agreements	Uncertain
Substantially reduce corruption and bribery in all its forms	Uncertain

Cost of corruption per year

	US$ per citizen
Brazil	–
Bolivia	439
Colombia	177
Guatemala	194
Haiti	1 043
Panama	592
Mexico	–
Paraguay	988
Angola	375
Cameroon	321
Ethiopia	343
Gabon	953
Ghana	159
Kenya	141
Mali	682
Nigeria	736
South Africa	–
Uganda	375
Zambia	213
Egypt	356
Iraq	808
Turkey	50
Bangladesh	1 151
China	–
India	87
Indonesia	916
Myanmar	773
Pakistan	537
Philippines	393
Thailand	60
Vietnam	240

2014 $-value, 2005 data from A Dreher et al (2005)

11. HEALTH SYSTEMS
STRENGTHEN HEALTH SYSTEMS TO REDUCE PREMATURE DEATHS

Last year, life expectancy on the planet reached 70. This is remarkable progress – in 1900, life expectancy was about 30. Compared to a century ago, each of us has now been granted more than two lifetimes.

But there are still many health problems we could tackle better. The question is which we should focus on.

There are lots of excellent proposals to address particular health challenges, such as malaria, vaccinations or infant death. But focusing on these single issues that have lots of media attention and straightforward solutions easily means forgetting about the many other ailments. Our new peer-reviewed reports suggest that we should look at strengthening the entire health system. Compare this to low-income countries, where the world's poorest one billion live. These countries spend a measly $14 per person on public health care. Not surprisingly, spending just a little more could do a lot of good.

This year, 9 million people in low-income countries like Bangladesh, Uganda and Haiti will die before their 70th birthday. This will affect another 19 million in lower middle-income countries like India, Nigeria and Guatemala. But as countries get richer by 2030, they will also get healthier. It is estimated that by 2030, the total premature death will have dropped from 28 million to 24 million per year, despite the population having grown by almost a billion. Yet, we can do much better.

The Canadian authors of the study find it is possible to achieve a further reduction in mortality, resulting in a two-thirds drop from 2010 child mortality and a one-thirds drop from 2010 deaths from people between 5 and 69 years of age. In total, this would reduce deaths in the poor half of the world by another 7 million annually by 2030.

This would require increasing health spending from the current 2% of GDP to 5% of GDP. In low-income countries public health spending will have risen to $23 per person by 2030 because countries will be richer. But increasing it another $34 will allow us to avoid an extra 2 million deaths each year. For lower middle income countries, the average public health expenditure will be $85 per person, but increasing this another $128 will save almost 5 million more lives by 2030.

Because we're talking about helping half the world's population, this is not cheap. Total extra costs will run to almost half a trillion dollars each year by 2030. Yet, it still compares favorably to the benefits of saving 7 million lives, both as measured in lost productivity and as the intrinsic value ascribed to human beings. The overall estimate shows that for every dollar spent, we will achieve $4 of human benefits. For the poorest one billion, because the spending is so much lower that there are many more low-hanging fruits, each dollar spent would do $13 worth of good.

This compares to some of the high-profile diseases like tuberculosis, which will do $43 worth of good for every dollar spent, or malaria, which will produce $36 of benefits for every dollar. These are higher, because it is very effective to save lives of children and young adults afflicted with easily curable diseases. Helping everyone through a more comprehensive health system is more just but also means dealing with less easy diseases and helping higher age groups, where you can save fewer life-years.

Of course, it's more complicated than just spending more money on cures; the funds have to be channeled into more trained staff, more clinics and more medicine, to be employed as effectively as possible in each area to reduce overall mortality (and also the wider burden of disease and disability). But the benefits of having better health provision are undeniable. Medical staff can not only provide continuing care and prevent or treat the normal range of illnesses and ensure safer births, but they are in a position to react to emergencies as they arise.

For example, a considerable number of people die from injuries each year, and the team of economists reckons that this number could also be reduced by a third. The Ebola outbreak in West Africa is another clear example. The countries which are suffering most have very poor general health provision and large amounts of international assistance are being poured in to halt the epidemic. With a properly functioning local health service, the disease may never have got a hold in the first place.

There are plenty of potentially very good health targets proposed as priorities for the next 15 years, focusing on HIV, malaria, TB and infant mortality in particular. All are worthy of our attention, but a good case has been made for simply strengthening health services to achieve an overall cut in premature death.

Target	Costs in 2030 ($b)	Benefits in 2030 ($b)	Benefit for every dollar spent
By 2030, reduce premature mortality by 40% in low income countries (LICs)	$42	$584	$13
By 2030, reduce premature mortality by 40% in lower-middle-income countries (LMIs)	$402	$1,080	$3
By 2030, reduce premature mortality by 40% in LICs and LMIs	$444	$1,664	$4

Public Health Spending and Life Expectancy

	Public health spending US$ per person	Public health spending % GDP	Life expectancy
Brazil	490	4%	74
Chile	536	3%	80
Colombia	402	5%	74
Costa Rica	710	7%	80
Ecuador	162	3%	76
Guatemala	80	2%	72
Mexico	320	3%	77
Peru	199	3%	75
Ethiopia	9	2%	63
Ghana	47	3%	61
Kenya	17	1%	61
Mali	16	2%	55
Mozambique	17	3%	50
Nigeria	29	1%	52
Rwanda	38	6%	63
South Africa	309	5%	56
Tanzania	16	2%	61
Uganda	10	2%	59
Zambia	62	3%	57
Egypt	59	2%	71
Iran	198	4%	74
Turkey	491	4%	75
Bangladesh	9	1%	70
China	180	3%	75
India	20	1%	66
Indonesia	43	1%	71
Nepal	14	2%	68
Pakistan	12	1%	66
Philippines	45	2%	69
Thailand	164	3%	74
Vietnam	44	2%	76

2012 data from The World Bank and WHO

12. ILLICIT FINANCIAL FLOWS
DIRTY DEVELOPMENT MONEY

In 2011, Global Financial Integrity estimated the developing world lost almost a trillion dollars[1], illegally transferred to the developed world. In Africa, 20 countries have lost more than 10% of their GDPs every year since 1980 to illicit financial flows. The illicit flows are ten times the current level of international aid. Africa has been a net creditor to the world over the period 1980-2009 to the tune of maybe $1.4 trillion.[2]

And this problem affects almost all countries. In 2011, Latin America lost more than $116 billion. Each year, Latin America lose about 2.6% of the region's GDP. Chile loses more than $5 billion each year.

Economist Alex Cobham, research fellow at the Center for Global Development, argues that we should definitely think about illicit financial transfers when thinking about the next 15 years.

Illicit flows are illegal when they are simple money laundering or dictators stealing from the national budgets. But 80% are tax avoidance, transferring money out of the country by *under*-invoicing exports or *over*-invoicing imports. Recent headlines about the European tax arrangements of companies such as Amazon, Starbucks and Google have raised the profile of this issue.

So, what should we do? Economist Alex Cobham, research fellow at the Center for Global Development, proposes that one of the key targets for the next global goals should be "Make all beneficial ownership information publicly available" This would make illicit financial flows much harder to accomplish (and much easier to spot). If such a proposal gave just a 10% reduction in the average losses of illicit financial flows in the decade from 2002, the benefit would be $768bn, but reducing current losses by half would raise this to a staggering $7.5tn.

---

1 All numbers from http://bit.ly/1gHLjvG, here S$946.7 billion in 2011, page ix.
2 From Illicit Financial Flows and the Problem of Net Resource Transfers from Africa: 1980-2009, http://bit.ly/1CAncro.

A wide range of costs of compliance have also been estimated, but even using the highest of these ($66bn) with the lowest benefit scenario means it pays off handsomely. For every dollar spent, it will do 13 dollars of good. Greater success and lower costs could see this rising to the thousands of dollars for each dollar spent. For his two other proposals – automatic exchange of tax information between different jurisdictions and country-by-country reporting by multinationals – it is much harder to define the benefits, but they are likely to be highly cost-effective measures.

But – and there's always a but – these transparency proposals have to be pretty well universally adhered to if there is to be a substantial impact, otherwise more money will simply pass through other channels which remain open. The precedent of the existing anti-money laundering framework is not reassuring.

This system is universally accepted and most countries obey the letter of the law without in practice stemming the flow of illegal money. Even major international banks are sometimes found to have flagrantly flouted the rules. However, these systems are complex and varied and the wider transparency proposals have the benefit of greater simplicity, so perhaps we should be more optimistic about them.

Hence, even though we can't hope to meet all the new targets for 2015-2030, Cobham has made a strong argument for why Illicit Financial Flows should be on the agenda, and why dealing with them could do a lot of good per dollar spent.

IFF Targets	Benefit For Every Dollar
Reduce to zero the legal persons and arrangements for which beneficial ownership info is not publicly available.	$49
Reduce to zero the cross-border trade and investment relationships between jurisdictions for which there is no bilateral automatic exchange of tax information.	Likely To Be High
Reduce to zero the number of multinational businesses that do not report publicly on a country-by-country basis.	Likely To Be High

Illicit financial flows per year

	million US$
Brazil	19 269
Chile	4 520
Colombia	1 202
Costa Rica	8 065
Ecuador	1 151
Guatemala	1 754
Mexico	46 186
Peru	909
Ethiopia	2 024
Ghana	316
Kenya	86
Mali	375
Mozambique	87
Nigeria	14 227
Rwanda	211
South Africa	10 073
Tanzania	453
Uganda	739
Zambia	1 934
Egypt	3 588
Iran	0
Turkey	3 728
Bangladesh	1 608
China	107 557
India	34 393
Indonesia	18 183
Nepal	805
Pakistan	102
Philippines	8 887
Thailand	14 088
Vietnam	2 216

2002–2011 average from D Karr & B LeBlanc

13. INFANT MORTALITY AND MATERNAL HEALTH
HOW TO SAVE MORE THAN 14 MILLION NEWBORNS BY 2030

In a world where there are so many worthwhile targets demanding our attention, we need to focus on those where we have the best chance of doing the most good. How about saving more than 14 million newborns by 2030?[1] That's a pretty eye-catching figure, but one which the author of a new analysis for the Copenhagen Consensus believes is not only achievable, but also highly cost-effective.

Günther Fink, from the Harvard School of Public Health, is one of more than 60 expert economists my think tank has asked to make the case for a wide range of key targets which the world's governments and the UN are currently debating. These will shape global progress over the next 15 years, so it's important to get them right.

Is it really possible to make such a dramatic difference to the survival of newborn babies? Past experience would suggest that it is. UN figures show that nearly 18 million children round the world died before reaching the age of five in 1970, while in 2013 that figure had come down to just above 6 million. This is still way too high, of course, but it's nevertheless a very impressive figure, even more so when we realise that the number of births annually has increased during those forty years.

The problem is that the more progress you make, the harder the remaining targets are to reach. Much of the progress in controlling infant mortality since 1970 has been in areas such as controlling infectious diseases and improving nutrition. Progress in this should and will continue, but this won't be as rapid as before. It's a sobering thought that, with the current birth rate, under-5 mortality would still exceed 4 million each year even if all infectious diseases were eradicated. One of

---

1 Based on saving 1.93m in 2030, and linearly scaling up from zero in 2015, so 15*1.93m/2.

the biggest challenges going forward will be providing high quality care to newborns, particularly to those born too early and with low birth weight. Deaths in the first seven days after birth are virtually one third of all under-5 deaths, and premature birth is the biggest single cause, accounting for half of these.

As well as the perils of prematurity, birth complications and sepsis are significant causes of deaths of young babies. Proper care can have a really big impact, but it costs money to build more clinics and train and pay more doctors and nurses: about $14 billion a year to hit the target of a 70% reduction in neonatal deaths, according to estimates. That sounds a lot, but the benefits are much bigger at more than $120 billion annually. For each dollar spent, we will help the world's newborn about $9.[2]

Reducing infant mortality is not the only good target, of course. One which gets a lot of attention is access to contraception, which enables women to have children when the time is right for them, gives them better employment prospects and enables them to invest more in their children's future. A dollar spent on this could pay back perhaps 120-fold.

But while family planning is high profile, there are other good ways for the international community to invest in women's health. This was analyzed in another paper from Dara Lee Luca and colleagues from Harvard University. The fourth most common cancer among women globally is cervical cancer, with half a million cases diagnosed annually and more than 200,000 deaths each year. 85% of cases occur in the developing world, where it is actually the second deadliest cancer among women, after breast cancer. Its impact is particularly great because it also affects younger women who are raising and supporting families.

Fortunately, many of these cases are preventable, because nearly all are associated with a viral infection, and a vaccination is available. The vaccine is more expensive than most and three doses are needed, but in total, a course of treatment in developing countries would cost $25 per girl. Vaccinating 70% of girls in one cohort throughout most of the developing world would cost about $400 million, and would save 274,000 women from dying, often in the prime of their lives, from cervical cancer. For each dollar spent, we would do more than three dollars worth of good.

---

2 Based on the average of $5.7 and $11.7 or $8.75. $14bn*8.75 gives more than $120bn.

Health is obviously high on everyone's agenda, but the escalating costs in rich countries show there are no easy answers. Choosing the best targets for the international community to support between now and 2030 is going to be very important if we are to do the most good with the resources available. Dealing with neonatal deaths and cervical cancer could be two of the smart targets we should choose.

Target	Annual Costs ($b)	Annual Benefits ($b)	Benefit for Every Dollar spent
Universal access to sexual and reproductive health (SRH) services by 2030	$3.6	$433	$120
Reduce neo-natal (0-27 days) mortality by 70% (2013-2030)	$14	$132	$9
Diminish the lifetime risk of cervical cancer by 40% (representing nearly 3m avoided deaths)	$0.4	$1.4	$3

Under Age 5 Deaths

	1990	2013	2030
Brazil	217 862	41 206	36 599
Chile	5 737	2 014	1 065
Colombia	31 520	15 326	11 693
Costa Rica	1 435	714	446
Ecuador	17 341	7 358	4 096
Guatemala	26 630	14 685	8 977
Mexico	112 137	32 714	21 844
Peru	52 107	9 935	8 154
Ethiopia	446 726	195 504	143 064
Ghana	70 438	61 530	53 309
Kenya	96 060	105 859	95 437
Mali	91 052	82 267	112 171
Mozambique	135 155	82 891	86 403
Nigeria	851 797	804 429	748 989
Rwanda	49 682	21 684	19 952
South Africa	65 181	47 459	33 303
Tanzania	179 678	95 312	112 288
Uganda	145 837	101 552	116 852
Zambia	63 462	51 474	55 908
Egypt	153 965	41 514	26 192
Iran	107 272	24 738	12 169
Turkey	103 442	24 798	9 654
Bangladesh	531 423	129 433	53 622
China	1 643 985	235 612	150 192
India	3 333 151	1 340 055	871 677
Indonesia	387 165	136 371	90 449
Nepal	95 494	22 674	12 128
Pakistan	620 252	393 959	231 633
Philippines	119 241	70 987	53 365
Thailand	40 470	9 134	4 353
Vietnam	99 336	33 396	16 233

1990 & 2013 data from The World Bank, WHO and 2025-30 forecast from UN DESA

14. INFECTIOUS DISEASES
EBOLA KILLS FEWER
THAN AIDS, TB AND MALARIA.
WHAT SHOULD WE PRIORITIZE?

Ebola has gotten much of the attention in 2014, and it has killed about 8,000 people. Over the same period of time, however, about 4 million people died from AIDS, tuberculosis (TB) and malaria. The truth is that despite great progress in healthcare, much of the world is still blighted by preventable disease, with the poorest people suffering the most. The good news is that tackling these diseases turn out to be an extraordinarily good investment.

It may sound cold-hearted to set health priorities based on cost-effectiveness, but it's actually the best way to do the most good in the world with limited resources.

Health is a big topic, and we've had the perspectives of five expert groups plus a number of commentaries. The case they make for tackling killer diseases is a strong one. Take TB. Two billion people worldwide carry the bacterium that causes it, and 1 in 10 of them will go on to develop the disease. TB probably killed about 100 million people over the 20th century[1], and was one of the major killers before antibiotics became available. The success of this treatment has almost wiped out TB in rich countries, but it continues to be a disease of the poor, and kills about 1.5 million each year. The global risk of dying from TB has been reduced by more than one-third over the past twenty years, and since 1995, the progress is estimated to have saved 37 million people from dying. Yet, further progress has been hampered by weak health systems, poverty and multi-drug resistant strains of TB. Despite the toll it takes, TB treatment receives just 4% of total development assistance spent on health, compared with 25% for HIV.

TB can be difficult to detect, particularly in countries with poor health systems, and the World Health Organization recommends a pre-

---

[1] http://www.informationisbeautiful.net/visualizations/20th-century-death/

ventative course of drugs, costing just $21 per person, for high-risk populations. Treatment is highly effective and on average can give people a further 20 years of productive life. Helping almost everyone who's sick will cost about $8 billion a year, but provide benefits worth almost $350 billion. Each dollar spent this way will generate $43 worth of benefits.

Malaria is another killer disease. 90% of those it kills are in sub-Saharan Africa, and 77% are children under five. By far the most effective treatment is to use a drug called artemisinin. Like all widely-used drugs, there is a danger that malarial parasites will develop resistance to it, so it is crucial to delay resistance by using artemisinin in combination with one or more other malaria medicines. In total, this will likely cost about half a billion dollars but have benefits of twenty billion dollars, or about $36 worth of benefits for each dollar spent.

But what about HIV/AIDS? Treatment with anti-retroviral drugs has made an enormous difference to people with HIV infection, but it continues to cause large-scale human suffering in sub-Saharan Africa, where 70% of the global population of HIV positive people live. Globally, 35 million people live with HIV. The team studying this disease argues that the current use of anti-retroviral drugs should be expanded – doubling the amount spent on it – to reach all those people with significantly weakened immune systems.

This is not a cheap option, needing another $10 billion annually, but reaching 90% of the target group of patients would save many lives and be cost-effective. Every dollar spent would give benefits (extra years of life) valued at $10. And this is not the only option. Male circumcision is a one-off treatment, which can reduce the transmission of HIV to men during intercourse by 60% and, with some delay, also reduce transmission to women. Although not as effective as widespread drug treatment, the cost would be about $30 million annually but provide benefits of almost a billion dollars per year. Each dollar spent would return $28 worth of benefits.

However, one of the economists working on this project has proposed a radically different approach. Her argument is that focusing on a handful of key diseases has created islands of excellence in a sea of dysfunction. Much better, she suggests, to build up strong health systems which can deal with *all* medical problems. The problem is that the cost is phenomenally higher and the efficiency per dollar likely much lower.

However, it is worth remembering that there are bigger problems than the 4 million killed by AIDS, TB and malaria – take working-age injury and trauma, which kills almost 6 million each year.

In the health sector, we are spoilt for choice of good projects to spend money efficiently – and transform people's lives. Now it's up to the world's governments to look at the evidence and make good choices on priorities for the next fifteen years. The lives of millions of people depend on it.

Disease	Target	Annual benefits ($m)	Annual costs ($m)	Benefit for Every Dollar Spent
Malaria	Delay artemisinin resistance greater than 1% and reduce malaria incidence by 50% between 2015 and 2025	$20,428	$570	$36
Tuberculosis	Reduce TB deaths by 95% and TB incidence by 90%	$344,647	$8,092	$43
HIV / AIDS	In hyper-endemic countries, attain circumcision coverage of at least 90% amongst HIV-negative adult men	$818	$30	$28
HIV / AIDS	In hyper-endemic countries, prioritize and achieve ART coverage of at least 90% amongst HIV-infected adults with a very weak immune system (i.e. CD4 count <350 cells/µL)	$10,277	$1,080	$10

Infectious diseases

	People living with HIV	Malaria cases	Tubercolosis deaths (non-HIV related)	Tubercolosis death risk reducition since 1990
Brazil	730 000	310 000	4 400	59%
Chile	38 000	–	41 000	84%
Colombia	140 000	97 000	58	29%
Costa Rica	7 600	8	4 000	–
Ecuador	37 000	640	320	89%
Guatemala	53 000	8 700	250	84%
Mexico	180 000	1 000	2 200	77%
Peru	65 000	57 000	2 300	77%
Ethiopia	790 000	4 200 000	30 000	64%
Ghana	220 000	6 900 000	1 100	90%
Kenya	1 600 000	3 500 000	9 100	46%
Mali	97 000	3 000 000	1 600	47%
Mozambique	1 600 000	7 000 000	18 000	42%
Nigeria	3 200 000	48 000 000	160 000	5%
Rwanda	200 000	650 000	810	1/3 increase
South Africa	6 300 000	17 000	25 000	6%
Tanzania	1 400 000	8 300 000	6 000	74%
Uganda	1 600 000	8 900 000	4 100	87%
Zambia	1 100 000	3 700 000	3 600	69%
Egypt	7 400	–	550	81%
Iran	70 000	930	2 500	36%
Turkey	–	0	310	93%
Bangladesh	9 500	610 000	80 000	36%
China	–	6 800	770	68%
India	2 100 000	19 000 000	240 000	50%
Indonesia	640 000	5 600 000	64 000	64%
Nepal	39 000	17 000	4 600	67%
Pakistan	68 000	3 500 000	49 000	61%
Philippines	–	23 000	27 000	51%
Thailand	440 000	140 000	8 100	37%
Vietnam	250 000	27 000	17 000	63%

2013 data from WHO

15. INFRASTRUCTURE
THE DIGITAL ROAD FROM POVERTY

Where should the global community focus its attention over the next fifteen years? Health, nutrition and education may seem like obvious top priorities but, more surprisingly, there is also a strong case for broadband access to be considered. Tripling mobile internet access to 60% over the next 15 years could make the developing world $22 trillion richer. And such improvement in the lives and earning potential of poor people could indirectly help with the other challenges; more prosperous people tend to be healthier, better fed and better educated.

Professor Emmanuelle Auriol and Alexia Lee González Fanfalone from the Toulouse School of Economics suggest in a new analysis that broadband could very well be one of the best investments for the future.

Clearly, the rapid rollout of broadband services has transformed the lives of people in the industrialized world and there is every reason to expect that developing countries could benefit at least as much. Access to market information can make sure farmers know the market price for their surplus crops so they are not cheated by unscrupulous traders, and fishermen can land their catch at the port offering the best price. Economic models project that tripling mobile broadband coverage in the developing world could add up to $400 billion to global GDP and create over 10 million direct jobs.

A World Bank study showed that a 10% increase in broadband penetration increased GDP growth by 1.4% in low to medium income countries. This is important, because the digital divide among developed and developing regions of the world still persists and closing it could give a big boost to development. For example, while mobile broadband is used by over 83% of people in the industrialized world, penetration is only 21% in developing countries.

While governments in Europe and elsewhere continue to invest in faster and better broadband, the biggest benefits will always come from providing Internet connection to people who don't already have it, most of whom live in developing and emerging countries. Here, the developing world can leap-frog industrialized countries, eschew expensive fiber-optic cables in what is called the "last mile" or access part of the network, and go straight to mobile broadband.

Mobile phone use is already spreading rapidly in developing countries, avoiding the need for old-style fixed infrastructure, and data services can use the same system. In China, three quarters of Internet users access it via mobile phones already, and in Ethiopia and Uganda, four out of five use the mobile internet. Thus rolling out mobile broadband seems a cost effective solution given its pervasiveness and recent technological advances in mobile networks.

The study shows that increasing mobile broadband about three-fold in developing regions – from 21 to 60% -- will have a significant cost (about $1.3 trillion). This is simply the cost of the extra infrastructure needed to hook up about three billion more connections to the internet. However, it will also increase GDP growth. By 2020, the benefits would be almost half a trillion annually, and these would increase further towards 2030. Over the coming decades the total benefit would reach about $22 trillion. For every dollar spent on mobile broadband, the academics estimate a benefit of $17 dollars. Investing in mobile broadband for the developing world looks like a really smart move.

If the goal of 60% broadband by 2030 were achieved, it would make each person in the developing world almost $11,000 richer on average.

Broadband is such an important enabling technology that it is difficult to estimate the complete impact on the economy, which will vary with local circumstances. What the study does show, though, is that rolling out Internet access is money very well spent. Jobs are created directly in the organisation providing the network and indirectly in the supply chain. Once in place, broadband helps to create more jobs in the wider economy. Companies become more efficient and innovative. All these factors increase the rate of economic growth, and therefore make a strong case for governments to include broadband access to the next set of global targets.

Target	Discounted Benefits ($B) 2015-2030	Discounted Cost ($B) 2015-2030	Benefit For Every Dollar Spent
Increase World fixed broadband penetration by three-fold from 2014 levels (from 10% to 30% in 2030)	$35,930	$1,735	$21
Increase Developing countries' fixed broadband penetration by approx. three-fold from 2014 levels (from 6% to 20% in 2030)	$21,279	$1,031	$21
Increase World mobile broadband penetration by approx. three-fold from 2014 levels (from 32% to 90% in 2030)	$37,659	$2,203	$17
Increase Developing countries' mobile broadband penetration by approx. three-fold (from 21% in 2014 to 60% in 2030)	$21,578	$1,260	$17
Increase World penetration of Fixed+ Mobile Broadband from 42% in 2014 to 100% 2030 (assuming to reach the target with 1/3 of fixed lines and 2/3 of mobile connections)	$38,050	$3,161	$12
Increase Developing countries' penetration of Fixed+ Mobile Broadband from 27% in 2014 to 80% in 2030 (reaching the target with 1/3 of fixed lines and 2/3 of mobile connections)	$21,891	$2,431	$9
Universal fixed broadband penetration by the year 2030	$38,103	$7,343	$5
Universal mobile broadband penetration by the year 2030	$38,072	$2,523	$15

Mobile broadband penetration

	Subscriptions per 100 inhabitants
Brazil	52
Chile	36
Colombia	8
Costa Rica	72
Ecuador	26
Guatemala	4
Mexico	–
Peru	3
Botswana	74
Ethiopia	5
Ghana	40
Kenya	3
Mali	2
Nigeria	10
Rwanda	6
South Africa	–
Tanzania	3
Zambia	1
Zimbabwe	38
Egypt	31
Iran	1
Turkey	32
Bangladesh	0
China	21
India	3
Indonesia	–
Malaysia	13
Nepal	13
Pakistan	1
Philippines	20
Thailand	52

2013 data from The Broadband Commission

16. NON-COMMUNICABLE DISEASES
STROKES, HEART ATTACKS AND CANCER: SAVE 5M LIVES EACH YEAR

In rich countries, the biggest health concerns are diseases such as cancer, stroke and cardiovascular and lung complaints, together classed as non-communicable diseases (because they are not caused by bacteria or viruses and cannot be passed between individuals). In the developing world, people often assume that the biggest threat to life comes from diseases like TB, dysentery, AIDS or malaria. But, while these are still big problems, non-communicable diseases (NCDs) are also a growing problem in poorer countries.

The good news is that starting a program of interventions now could save five million premature deaths by 2030. Not only that, but this program would be an excellent use of scarce funding: each dollar spent would give benefits valued at $12. Particular components to reduce blood pressure or cut smoking could pay pack two or three time as much. This looks like a win-win situation – millions of people could have their health improved and their lives extended, and doing this would be one of the better ways of using the world's limited resources.

This is the argument made in a new paper written by Rachel Nugent of the University of Washington. Hers is one of a series commissioned by my think tank, the Copenhagen Consensus Center, from over 60 teams of top economists. The idea is to be able to compare a wide range of proposed targets for the global community to focus on over the coming fifteen years. An economic analysis of costs and benefits sets a level playing field so that the final choice will be of a set of targets which have the best chance of doing the most good for the world by 2030.

Professor Nugent looks at the target of reducing premature deaths from NCDs by a third by 2030. This is a pretty demanding target, because premature death rates are already quite low in the developed world, and most of the deaths below age 70 occur in poorer countries. And the problem is accelerating. The number of people affected by these diseases is set to increase by 17% over the next ten years, and by 27% in Africa, the one region where NCDs are not yet (quite) the major cause of death. A clear illustration of the problem is in Mexico, where deaths from NCDs went from just under half to three quarters of total deaths between 1980 and 2009.

So, what can we do about this big and growing problem? Because lifestyle is the major factor in most of these diseases, there have to be sustained, long-term changes in behaviour to make a difference. Fortunately, there are many quite straightforward things which can be done. Take high blood pressure, for example, considered as the 'silent killer' as it is a key risk factor for heart disease and stroke.

One of the simplest ways to reduce the incidence of hypertension across a population is to lower salt intake. Gradual reduction of the salt content in bread and other processed foods has been very successful in a number of countries, with very little sign of consumer resistance. Reducing salt intake by 30% over ten years is reckoned to save 6.7 million premature deaths (more than double this if deaths over 70 are also counted). It would also be a great use of resources, paying back at least $19 for every dollar spent.

But there are other simple interventions which would be even better. Rapidly treating heart attack sufferers is known to save lives. Simply giving victims aspirin as soon as possible would save over 55,000 lives at a cost of less than $15 per patient, including diagnosis and clinical visits. Every dollar spent would give benefits valued at least $31.

A third intervention, which would save many more lives, is increasing tobacco taxation by 125% to cut consumption by half. This approach would save 2.5 million lives by 2030 and, because a large part of the cost would be covered by tax revenue, the net cost would be only $1 billion. Every dollar spent would give a payback of at least $36, making it phenomenally cost-effective.

The choice that the global community is faced with when agreeing on the set of post-2015 goals is not an easy one, but it is vital that the targets included can do the most good and provide good value for money. Based on this analysis, reducing deaths from non-communicable diseases deserves very serious consideration.

Type	Target or Sub-target	Annual costs ($m)	Annual Benefits ($m)	Benefit for Every $ Spent	Deaths avoided in 2030 (m)
Target	By 2030, reduce premature death from non-communicable diseases by 29% in LMICs	$8,563	$153,668	$18	5.02
Sub-target	Provide aspirin to 75% of those suffering from acute myocardial infraction	$27	$1,271	$63	0.06
Sub-target	Provide low-cost hypertension medication to 50% of medium- and-high risk patients	$500	$23,479	$47	0.77
Sub-target	Reduce salt intake by 30%	$638	$24,943	$39	0.82
Sub-target	Increase the price of tobacco by 125%	$3,548	$76,537	$22	2.50
Sub-target	Provide preventive drug therapy to 70% of those at high risk of heart disease	$3,850	$26,990	$7	0.88

Raised blood pressure, tobacco deaths and NCD rising cause of deaths

	Raised blood preassure among adults	Tobacco smoking cause of over age 30 deaths	Non-communicable disease cause of total deaths
Brazil	42%	18%	74%
Chile	43%	16%	81%
Colombia	40%	19%	68%
Costa Rica	38%	11%	80%
Ecuador	39%	9%	65%
Guatemala	36%	6%	48%
Mexico	36%	12%	77%
Peru	34%	7%	62%
Ethiopia	41%	3%	30%
Ghana	42%	4%	38%
Kenya	45%	4%	22%
Mali	41%	5%	22%
Mozambique	51%	5%	20%
Nigeria	49%	3%	20%
Rwanda	49%	9%	29%
South Africa	46%	12%	34%
Tanzania	45%	4%	22%
Uganda	49%	5%	22%
Zambia	48%	6%	22%
Egypt	38%	17%	82%
Iran	39%	16%	76%
Turkey	36%	39%	85%
Bangladesh	39%	20%	60%
China	39%	24%	85%
India	35%	20%	53%
Indonesia	41%	24%	65%
Nepal	39%	20%	49%
Pakistan	40%	19%	50%
Philippines	37%	29%	63%
Thailand	34%	22%	70%
Vietnam	37%	26%	72%

2008 data from WHO and 2010 data from Global Burden of Disease Study

17. NUTRITION
FEEDING PEOPLE IS SMART

The world faces many problems, and feeding a growing population adequately is certainly one of them. The good news is that we are well on track to halving the proportion of people suffering chronic hunger between 1990 and 2015. The bad news is that still leaves over 800 million people who go to bed hungry every night. Unfortunately, there are no easy ways to solve this problem quickly, but there are smart ways to use resources to do a lot of good both now and in the long term.

Both children and adults need a good quality diet, but feeding young children well makes a big difference for their entire lives. The first 1,000 days of a child's life – from conception to age two – are vital for proper development. Poorly nourished infants don't grow as tall as their peers, and measuring the proportion of stunting (being smaller than the expected height for age) is a simple way of checking for malnourishment. These children don't just fail to thrive physically; they also fall behind better-fed ones in developing cognitive skills. This lack of development has real long-term consequences. Stunted children do less well at school and lead poorer adult lives.

Although there are lots of factors to take into account, the best basis for comparing competing targets on a level playing field is an economic assessment of costs and benefits. Most people would feel that feeding people properly – particularly young children – is something we simply have to tackle. And it turns out that what looks like a good idea morally is also really good economically. Good nutrition helps children develop properly and produces people who are able to make the best of all the opportunities which come their way.

The difference is dramatic, and well illustrated by a follow-up to an experiment in Guatemala. Starting in 1969, preschool children in several villages were given a nutritionally enhanced diet and compared with similar children in neighboring communities, who got a less nutritionally useful diet. Going back to these same children 35 years later, when they were mature adults, showed some startling differences. The well-nourished children were not stunted by age three, stayed in school longer and developed better cognitive skills as adults. They were more likely to be employed and earned higher wages; their better physical and mental development made them more suitable for both skilled manual and white-collar jobs. A study in Brazil, for example, showed that just a 1% increase in height raised average adult male earnings by 2.4%.

In Guatemala, the children who were better nourished, turned out to have a much higher income as adults, compared to the control group. They had a 66% higher household consumption, an impressive improvement in quality of life from simple interventions in childhood. Spending a small amount – just $96 in total – on providing nutritional supplements, improving the balance of the diet and deworming pays back handsomely. Over a working life, between the ages of 21 and 50, we can expect that a dollar spent on early childhood nutrition will on average do about $45 worth of good over a wide range of low- and middle-income countries. That makes it a truly phenomenal use of money.

The great thing about feeding infants well is that it starts a virtuous circle, with increasing benefits for succeeding generations. Good childhood nutrition produces people who can contribute more and help boost economic growth and can themselves bring up well-fed, healthy children. Healthy children grow up to be healthy, more productive adults who bring up the next generation to be even better fed, better educated and more productive.

Feeding people properly – and starting early – is not just a moral imperative; it also makes a lot of economic sense. That's the message that the world's governments and the UN will hear as they make their choice of targets for the post-2015 period.

Target	Benefit Per Child	Cost Per Child	Benefit For Every $ Spent
Reduce by 40% the number of children who are stunted.	$4,365	$97	$45

Prevalence of child malnutrition and intervention benefits

	Stunted children under age 5		Social and economic benefit per $1 spent on better nutrition
Brazil	7%	2007	
Chile	2%	2008	
Colombia	13%	2010	
Costa Rica	6%	2008	
Ecuador	29%	2004	
Guatemala	48%	2009	
Mexico	14%	2012	
Peru	28%	2008	
Botswana	44%	2011	$26
Ethiopia	29%	2008	
Ghana	35%	2009	$41
Kenya	39%	2006	
Mali	43%	2011	
Nigeria	36%	2011	$59
Rwanda	44%	2010	
South Africa	24%	2008	
Tanzania	43%	2010	$35
Zambia	34%	2011	$31
Zimbabwe	46%	2007	
Egypt	31%	2008	
Iran	7%	2004	
Turkey	16%	2004	
Bangladesh	41%	2011	$43
China	9%	2010	
India	48%	2006	$93
Indonesia	39%	2010	$115
Malaysia	41%	2011	$31
Nepal	43%	2011	$70
Pakistan	34%	2011	$105
Philippines	16%	2006	
Thailand	23%	2010	$85

Latest year available from The World Bank and 2015 data S Horton & J Hoddinott

18. POPULATION AND DEMOGRAPHY
THE POPULATION CHALLENGE

Start talking about the population problem, and most people assume you mean the continuing rapid increase in parts of the developing world. But, despite the headlines, the rate of growth is falling and numbers are set to plateau later this century. There is, however, a different problem which rich economies are facing right now and which will confront even today's poor countries before too long: a shrinking and ageing population.

We cannot afford to ignore the fact that the UN estimates there will be 2.4 billion more mouths to feed by mid-century, but neither can we be complacent about this major shift in demographics.

Birth rates in rich countries have fallen so low that populations are shrinking. At the same time, of course, they are ageing; the number of older people is rising fast because life expectancy has increased so much (surely a good news story). But this leads to the very real problem of more and more old people having to be supported by fewer and fewer people of working age.

Meanwhile, in developing countries, there is the opposite problem of too many young people without good jobs (or without any jobs). Those youngsters are going to be part of their own country's demographic transition as they age, but for now they need work.

Fortunately, there is a potential win-win solution available right now. Easing restrictions on migration allows young people from developing countries to expand workforces in industrialized economies and pay the taxes which help to fund services for the elderly. These workers would also send remittances to their home countries to help their families there.

The potential benefits of this are enormous: a modest 3% increase in the developed country workforce could give more benefits than removing all remaining trade barriers. And the costs are quite small: every dollar invested in achieving this would pay back nearly fifty-fold, making this a phenomenally good use of resources.

While this is great, we cannot ignore the rising global population. This is already a problem if we see a peak of about nine billion this century, as is widely projected. This suggests that there could be 12 billion or more people by the end of the century, with sub-Saharan Africa – persistently the poorest region – driving the growth.

Finding a good way to slow this down is important, and our economists believe that this is not only possible but can be done very cost-effectively. The key to this problem is ready access to modern contraception so that women can plan their families. The cost of this is not that high, but the benefits would be enormous. Providing contraception for the 215 million women who would like to avoid pregnancy but can't, would cost about $3.6 billion per year.

This would avoid human misery in the form of hundreds and thousands of deaths of newborns and their mothers, and 600,000 growing children would not lose their mothers. Putting this in economic terms may seem callous, but it's the only common basis for comparing competing projects. This protection of lives gives a benefit of about $145 billion per year.

And there is more good news. Better access to contraception would allow mothers to spend more time bringing up the children who are born, leading to better education. And with fewer kids, most of the population will be working, boosting the economy for a generation. This will likely mean an extra $288 billion per year. So a dollar spent on family planning programs yields about $120 in benefits, making it an astonishingly good investment.

Poor countries with stubbornly high birth rates are concentrated in Africa. These high-fertility countries have only 18% of the world's population at present, but produce 38% of the babies. Reducing this through education and access to modern contraceptives would have real benefits for families, but the improvements can be even greater if there are investments which promote health and provide education.

There is no silver bullet for sustainable development. A number of factors have to come together to improve the lot of the world's poorest, and that's why the economic analysis we are promoting is so important. There are always constraints on money and trained people, and analysing the costs and benefits can help to make sure limited resources are focussed on key priorities which, taken together, are likely to do the most good.

Population and Demography Targets	Annual Benefits ($B)	Annual Costs ($B)	Benefit for Every $ Spent
Universal access to sexual and reproductive health (SRH) services by 2030 AND eliminate unmet need for modern contraception by 2040.	$432	$3.6	$120
Reduce barriers to migration within low- and middle-income countries, as well as between low and middle-income countries and high-income countries.			>$45
Eliminate age-based eligibility criteria for retirement.			High
Promote more efficient and more equitable urbanization.			High
Increase low fertility in high-income countries.			<$1
Maintain and expand public pension eligibility at "relatively young" old ages.			Low

Children per woman, and people over age 65

	Fertility rate 1970	Fertility rate 2013	Over age 65 in 2015	Over age 65 in 2050
Brazil	5,0	1,8	16 330 000	52 008 000
Chile	4,0	1,8	1 894 000	5 123 000
Colombia	5,6	2,3	3 282 000	11 384 000
Costa Rica	5,0	1,8	376 000	1 427 000
Ecuador	6,1	2,6	1 109 000	3 899 000
Guatemala	6,2	3,8	758 000	2 712 000
Mexico	6,7	2,2	8 506 000	31 542 000
Peru	6,3	2,4	2 087 000	7 236 000
Ethiopia	7,0	4,6	3 447 000	12 973 000
Ghana	7,0	3,9	927 000	3 095 000
Kenya	8,1	4,5	1 290 000	6 097 000
Mali	6,9	6,9	436 000	1 471 000
Mozambique	6,6	5,3	897 000	2 427 000
Nigeria	6,5	6,0	4 986 000	16 627 000
Rwanda	8,2	4,6	311 000	1 733 000
South Africa	5,6	2,4	3 061 000	6 667 000
Uganda	7,1	6,0	967 000	4 180 000
Tanzania	6,8	5,3	1 697 000	6 295 000
Zambia	7,4	5,7	400 000	1 768 000
Egypt	5,9	2,8	5 025 000	14 969 000
Iran	6,4	1,9	4 390 000	21 595 000
Turkey	5,6	2,1	5 906 000	20 048 000
Bangladesh	6,9	2,2	7 794 000	32 729 000
China	5,5	1,7	132 457 000	331 314 000
India	5,5	2,5	70 059 000	205 752 000
Indonesia	5,5	2,4	13 875 000	50 725 000
Nepal	6,0	2,4	1 509 000	4 610 000
Pakistan	6,6	3,3	8 298 000	25 969 000
Philippines	6,3	3,1	4 155 000	14 628 000
Thailand	5,6	1,4	7 038 000	18 746 000
Vietnam	6,5	1,8	6 343 000	23 911 000

Data from The World Bank and UN DESA

19. POVERTY
SMART WAYS TO TACKLE POVERTY

Extreme poverty – by current reckoning, living on less than $1.25 a day – is a continuing problem for far too many people today.

It is also arguably one of the most important challenges to address because more prosperous people can afford more to eat, get better access to education and healthcare and generally live better lives. So it's good to see that excellent progress has been made in poverty reduction in recent years. The proportion of people in developing countries living in poverty more than halved between 1990 and 2010.

Globally, according to the World Bank, just over one billion people continue to live in poverty, although that's down from 1.9 billion in 1990. The big question now is whether this rapid improvement can be maintained so that we can truly make poverty history.

This is the question which Professor John Gibson of the University of Waikato sets out to answer in a paper commissioned by my think tank, the Copenhagen Consensus Center.

The obvious solution is probably not to address poverty head-on but focus on another policy that could help dramatically: free trade. The costs of successfully completing the Doha round of World Trade Organization talks would generate more than 2,000 times their value in benefits for developing countries and lift 160 million out of poverty.

However, this policy has also turned out to be very hard to implement, and Doha is languishing.

Gibson points out that already for the MDGs in 2000, a number of alternative targets were assessed and rejected in favor of a simple one: halving the rate of absolute poverty. He argues that this kind of target is still the most sensible one.

However, any target can sound deceptively simple but measuring progress – or even setting a reliable baseline – can be fraught with difficulty. Collecting reliable statistical data is almost impossible in countries with little survey infrastructure, the very places where poverty is still a big problem. And, if we can't measure it, we don't know if resources are being used properly.

The best which can be done is to take figures where they *are* available and draw whatever broader lessons we can. This is possible for Vietnam, which has made astonishing progress in recent years. In 1993, 64% of the population were below the poverty line; by 2010 this had fallen to just 5%. The benefits are wide-ranging. Not only are people earning more and have better access to good nutrition but more prosperous people are typically better educated, live longer and can make a bigger contribution to the wider economy. We can estimate the lowest cost for taking people out of poverty as the sum of money needed to plug their poverty gap. It turns out that each dollar transferred pays back 6-9 dollars in overall benefits, both measured in increased longevity, better education and higher incomes.

This, however, assumes that money can be perfectly targeted but this is an impossible task. Some of the money will be misused and some lost, so the true payback may be reduced by half, to perhaps 4-6 dollars for each one spent. The other important point is that the tremendous progress made in a range of East Asian countries (including Vietnam) in the recent past is due to a number of factors unlikely to come together elsewhere. This is particularly true of sub-Saharan Africa, where poverty is becoming concentrated although in the mid-1980s rates of poverty were very similar in both regions. Many East Asian countries can be thought of as states with the capacity to make institutional reforms to boost growth. There are unfortunately few African states in a similar position.

Another important factor at play in East Asia is the simple fact that the staple food is rice. As prosperity has increased and more wheat and meat have been eaten, rice has become cheaper for those poor who depend most on it. In African countries where there is much more dependence on wheat and maize, the demand for these grains for animal feed and biofuels pushes the price up. This doesn't mean we should give up on other regions but we have to recognize the difficulty of maintaining the rapid rate of global poverty reduction seen over the last two decades.

Poverty is a complex issue but experience shows that plenty can be done. Free trade, for one, can boost the growth of developing economies and provide more jobs. Freer migration could also be a great way to raise individual incomes. Investing in smart programs can help millions of people out of poverty.

Target	Benefit for every $ spent
Eliminate extreme poverty.	$5
Cover x% of people who are poor and vulnerable with social protection systems.	<$1
Build resilience of the poor and reduce by x% deaths and economic losses related to disasters.	<$1
Ensure equality of economic opportunity for all women and men, including secure rights to own land, property and other productive assets and access to financial services for all women and men.	Varies by sector
Achieve full and productive employment for all, including women and young people.	<$1
Every country will monitor the wellbeing of its citizenry. with improved measurements and reporting of life satisfaction.	<$1

Poverty, and extreme poverty (under $1.25 per day)

	Number of poor people at national poverty line	Recent year	Extreme poverty 1990	Extreme poverty 2010
Brazil	17 832 211	2013	17%	5%
Chile	2 492 417	2011	5%	1%
Colombia	14 786 350	2013	5%	8%
Costa Rica	1 091 365	2014	8%	3%
Ecuador	4 028 897	2013	14%	5%
Guatemala	7 897 432	2011	37%	4%
Mexico	63 203 230	2012	4%	1%
Peru	7 259 769	2013	14%	5%
Botswana	26 460 347	2011	62%	31%
Ethiopia	–		50%	22%
Ghana	–		36%	40%
Kenya	6 097 879	2010	85%	50%
Mali	12 778 481	2009	81%	61%
Nigeria	73 465 579	2010	60%	68%
Rwanda	5 003 797	2011	67%	63%
South Africa	23 468 718	2011	22%	14%
Tanzania	13 474 836	2012	70%	63%
Zambia	8 051 760	2009	69%	34%
Zimbabwe	7 996 276	2010	54%	74%
Egypt	20 006 901	2011	5%	1%
Iran	–		4%	1%
Turkey	1 701 934	2012	2%	1%
Bangladesh	47 619 637	2010	68%	43%
China	–		60%	12%
India	270 834 394	2012	51%	33%
Indonesia	28 234 816	2014	54%	16%
Malaysia	6 765 196	2010	75%	25%
Nepal	21 844 628	2011	62%	13%
Pakistan	24 370 105	2012	30%	18%
Philippines	8 788 076	2011	12%	0%
Thailand	15 268 939	2012	73%	14%

1990, 2010 & latest year available from The World Bank

20. SCIENCE AND TECHNOLOGY
HOW TO MAKE THE WORLD'S POOR $500 BILLION RICHER

There is a way to make the poor of this world $500 billion better off, but this solution is rarely discussed.

The reason technology is so important is that it makes people more productive, thereby boosting overall economic growth. Not just that but, once knowledge has been gained, it is embedded in society and can be used as a stepping stone for future growth. Countries with a reasonable technical or research and development base are in a better position to absorb and make the best use of more new technologies as they become available.

Professor Keith E. Maskus from University of Colorado has written an extensive paper on what works and how much good it will do. As he rightly points out, the UN's technology-related targets are simply too general and bland. Instead, using the economic literature, he puts forward two proposals.

The first proposal is straight-forward: if our goal is to get more technology available for the poor, maybe we should simply increase investment in research and development (R&D), especially in the developing world.

The point is the benefits from R&D do not just go to the company doing it; there are also broader societal benefits as productivity gains occur elsewhere in the economy and other people learn on the job or see the possibility for more innovation. After Apple produced an innovative touch screen on its first iPhone, the knowledge is now available to lots of products in many different areas.

This broader benefit justifies governments supporting research, either through tax credits or direct government spending on research in public institutions. Right now, the developing countries spend just 0.2% of their GDP on R&D and perhaps 0.3% in 2030. If we instead aim at 0.5% of GDP by 2030, this would naturally increase the direct government costs, but it would also increase the long-run technological innovation and capabilities.

The models estimate in total, that for every dollar spent, we could likely end up doing $3 worth of good. That is not bad.

However, there is another, and much more effective way to increase technological capabilities in low-income countries. Instead of focusing on innovating more technology to make people more productive, we could focus on getting more *people* to places where they would be productive.

While allowing the free mobility of goods (free trade) can add several percentage points to global GDP, we have long known that free mobility of *people* could add anywhere from 67-147% to global GDP. Allowing free mobility could essentially *double* the world's income.

This is because people in poor areas are not inherently unproductive but their circumstances mostly make them unproductive. So, if they were to migrate, from say, Guatemala to the US, they would become much more productive.

Of course, absolutely free mobility would result in a massive relocation from poor to rich countries, which would likely engender huge political issues. But professor Maskus suggests that we could start off with a modest goal of increasing current skilled migration by 5-20% with 10-year visas. Since we have the best models for the Americas, he estimates the outcome for this region, but it is likely the results can scale for the rest of the world.

5% increase in skilled migration would mean an extra 136,000 managerial and technical workers, with 97,000 going to the US, 13,000 going to Canada and 7,000 each to Argentina and Mexico. Although other research shows migrants would only become half or less as productive as Americans, this would still make them much better off. The model shows they would earn $15 billion more over the next 25 years. Moreover, as they would bring with them new ideas and concepts, they will increase productivity in the US and elsewhere by $1.5 billion.

Of course, this will also mean an outflow of skilled workers from poorer countries. For instance, 30,000 people will leave Mexico for 10 years. But they will send back money – about $3 billion in total. And while many worry about a 'brain drain', there is actually more evidence for a 'brain gain': If there is an opportunity to go abroad and make more money as a doctor or engineer, it will induce more young to invest in a professional education, meaning more doctors and technicians in the long run. And as these skilled professionals come back after 10 years, they will also bring back new ideas and higher productivity.

In total, the costs, mostly in lost tax revenue are significantly outweighed by the gains. For every dollar spent, this target could do 10-20 dollars worth of good. With the Americas making up one-third of the global economy, the potential benefits could go as high as $500 billion. That should make the target of higher labor mobility a strong contender for the world's next set of goals.

Science and Technology Targets	Benefit for Every $ Spent
Expand open international circulation of skilled workers by 5-20% of current skilled migrants	$15
Increase developing country R&D spending of GDP to 0.5%, and emerging countries to raise their ratios to 1.5%	$3

BENEFITS OF INCREASED SKILLED LABOR MIGRATION WITHIN AMERICAS

	Skilled workers leaving for 10 year	Remittances US$ millions sent back	Total economic benefits US$ millions incl. productivity gains
Argentina	5 400	109	680
Brazil	5 800	149	6 978
Chile	6 200	63	354
Central America	8 300	291	1 495
Carribean	22 100	741	3 900
Mexico	36 400	1 248	6 978
Other South America	16 800	382	2 009

INCREASED SKILLED LABOR MIGRATION WITHIN AFRICA AND EUROPE

	Skilled workers leaving for 10 year	Remittances US$ millions sent back	Total economic benefits US$ millions incl. productivity gains
Botswana	16 000	940	3 053
Ethiopia	4 200	250	812
Ghana	6 900	410	1 332
Kenya	1 100	60	195
Mali	3 700	220	715
Nigeria	18 000	1 060	3 443
Rwanda	1 600	90	292
South Africa	15 900	1 060	3 423
Tanzania	9 000	530	1 721
Zambia	6 100	360	1 169
Zimbabwe	2 200	130	422
Egypt	23 800	1 590	5 134
Turkey	23 900	1 590	5 134

2015 data from K Maskus

21. TRADE
WHY EMBRACING FREER TRADE COULD BE OUR BEST CHANCE TO HELP THE WORLD'S POOR

With one simple policy – more free trade – we could make the world $500 trillion better off and lift 160 million people out of extreme poverty. If there is one question we have to ask ourselves, it is: why don't we?

As argued in a new paper by professor Kym Anderson of the University of Adelaide, reducing trade barriers not only makes the world richer, it is a great enabler for reducing poverty, curtailing hunger, improving health and restoring the environment.

Freer trade essentially means that each country can focus on doing what it does best, making all countries better off. Big strides have been made in liberalization since the Second World War, but the latest phase – the Doha Development Agenda – seems stalled, with little hope of a resolution. This is dreadful, in particular for developing countries, because two of the main areas where agreement is elusive are agriculture and textiles, both sectors where lower wage countries in the Tropics and sub-Tropics have comparative advantage.

Analysis shows that there would be substantial rewards for completing the Doha round. The direct economic benefits would be around 1.1% increase in global GDP. This sounds modest, but because it would impact the entire world economy, by 2030 we would every year be about $1.5 trillion richer.

But open economies grow faster as well. In the last 50 years, countries as diverse as South Korea, Chile and India have seen their rate of growth shoot up by 1.5% p.a. on average, shortly after liberalization. Globally, it is estimated the economy will grow by an extra 0.6% for the next decades. By 2030, such dynamic growth would make the world economy $11.5 trillion larger each year, essentially leaving us 10% more resources to fix all other problems.

And a large part of the benefit will go to the developing world, which by 2030 would see its economy $7 trillion larger each year. On average, the increased GDP is equivalent to $1,000 more for every person in the developing world.

By the end of the century, free trade could leave our grand kids twenty percent better off, or with a hundred trillion dollars more every year than they would otherwise have had.

For now, powerful vested interests make it difficult for politicians to compromise. The jobs that are lost from free trade are obvious and concentrated – witness Western farmers protesting losing their subsidies. But the benefits are less clear and spread out – for example, foods will be a bit cheaper for everyone, and third world farmers will see greater profits.

Yet, we need to keep a sense of proportion. There are real costs from free trade in terms of workers needing retraining and the provision of unemployment benefits. These outlays will occur mostly over the next decade and cost $100 to $300 billion. But the benefits will accrue for at least the next nine decades, and sum in present day dollars to $500 trillion. For every dollar spent, we will achieve more than $3,000 of benefits.

And this will have huge impacts for the world's poor. We know that economic growth has been one of the major drivers of poverty reduction – China's rapid growth over the past 30 years has pulled 680 million people out of poverty, the most ever achieved in human history.

Yet, we still have about 1.2 billion people living in abject poverty today. With future growth this number will likely be reduced to a still chokingly high 700 million by 2030. But if we achieve freer trade through the Doha round, the faster growth could lift an extra 160 million people out of poverty by 2030.

It is worth stepping back and realizing the amazing opportunity for the world. Yes, we should help with food, education, health and environment. But if we could just get it right on free trade, we could possibly do more good here than anywhere else – leaving the world $500 trillion better off, with 160 million fewer poor.

Trade Targets	Total Benefits ($trillion)	Total Costs ($trillion)	World Benefit for Every $ Spent	Developing Countries Benefit for Every $ Spent
Complete the languishing Doha Development Agenda process at the World Trade Organization.	$533	$0.28	$2,011	$3,426
Implement a free trade agreement between member states of the free trade area of the Asia Pacific.	$371	$0.22	$1,728	$2,559
Implement a free trade agreement between selected APEC countries (known as the Trans-Pacific Partnership).	$91	$0.07	$1,229	$1,870
Implement a free trade agreement between ASEAN countries and China, Japan and South Korea (known as ASEAN+3).	$243	$0.13	$1,914	$3,438

BENEFITS FROM FREER TRADE

	Extra US$ per person per year in 2030
Brazil	3 500
Chile	no estimate
Colombia	2 000
Costa Rica	2 500
Ecuador	1 500
Guatemala	900
Mexico	2 850
Peru	no estimate
Botswana	100
Ethiopia	400
Ghana	300
Kenya	200
Mali	150
Nigeria	750
Rwanda	150
South Africa	2 300
Tanzania	150
Zambia	150
Zimbabwe	500
Egypt	900
Iran	1 800
Turkey	3 250
Bangladesh	250
China	1 400
India	450
Indonesia	950
Malaysia	200
Nepal	350
Pakistan	700
Philippines	1 550
Thailand	450

2015 data from K Anderson

22. WATER AND SANITATION
INVESTMENTS IN WATER IN POOR NATIONS GIVE BIG BENEFITS

There are plenty of things, which those of us lucky enough to live in the industrialized world take for granted; running water and flush toilets are among the most basic of these. 2.5 billion – almost half the developing world – lack even a basic latrine[1] and 1 billion have to resort to what is politely known as open defecation.

750 million people have no access to any type of basic source of drinking water.[2] Each day, 136 million town dwellers spend more than 40 minutes each day to fetch water. Each day, more than 600 million in rural areas use more than an hour to fetch their water.[3]

The good news is that we can do something. Over the past 25 years, more than 2 billion have gained access to better water and almost 2 billion to sanitation.

Moreover, it turns out to be a good investment. Investing a dollar in basic sanitation can provide $3 worth of benefits. Basic water supply into the home can do even more good, giving more than $4 in benefits for each dollar spent. Getting rid of open defecation can help to the tune of $6 per dollar spent.

So, what is the case for prioritizing clean water and sanitation? The most obvious benefit comes in the form of better health. Providing even basic latrines and hand washing facilities can make a big impact on the spread of disease. There are a number of water-borne infectious diseases that could be curtailed. The biggest and deadliest are those that cause diarrhea, including cholera and a range of viral infections. These are a significant cause of death, particularly among young children, but infected adults may be too ill to work, and older children unfit to go to school.

1 http://bit.ly/1hYblqG
2 http://bit.ly/1hYblqG
3 from table p72-3 in http://bit.ly/1hYblqG

The other big benefit is time-saving. The analysis of the basic water supply and sanitation targets assumes that people in rural villages no longer have to spend an hour a day on average fetching water, but can collect the same amount in 20 minutes. In urban areas – which will continue to grow fast over coming decades – it is expected that people will halve the time needed to collect water from 40 to 20 minutes. For an American or European it may still sound onerous, but the time saving and health improvement which comes from even something as rudimentary as this would be an enormous benefit for hundreds of millions of people.

Because we will add an extra billion people to the global population over the next 15 years, getting water and sanitation to everyone will require a substantial effort. However, a team of economists from the World Bank has estimated that providing sanitation for 3 billion more people will cost about $31 billion annually. This is the cost of providing such low-cost solutions as pour-flush and dry pit latrines in rural areas and flush toilets to a septic tank in urban areas, shared by less than 30 people. Yet, the benefits will amount to $92 billion annually, about three-quarters of which are time benefits, and the remaining one-quarter are health benefits (it omits environmental benefits). This means that every dollar spent on sanitation will help the world's most vulnerable about $3, measured in better health and less time wasted.

Providing improved water to an extra 2.3 billion people will cost $14 billion annually. This doesn't mean industrialized world standard of piped water to every household, but simply providing a protected community source of water, such as a well, spring and borehole, or collected rainwater that can be reached within 30 minutes or less. Yet, again it will create much larger benefits, with less disease and death and with less wasted time. In all, the benefits are estimated at $52 billion annually, so that each dollar spent will generate $4 of benefits.

One stop on the way to better sanitation is simply avoiding open defecation in rural areas with shared latrine or communal toilets. Because this is even cheaper at $13 billion annually, each dollar can deliver a substantial benefit of $6.

In short, there is a strong case for investing in improved water supplies and sanitation. This would help half this world's population and benefit the poorest the most. The economic case is as strong as the moral one.

Target	Annual Cost $b	Annual Benefit $b	Benefit for every $ spent
Eliminate open defecation (rural only)	$13	$84	$6
Universal access to basic drinking water at home	$14	$52	$4
Universal access to basic sanitation at home	$31	$92	$3

Number of people without water and sanitation

	Lack basic water access	Lack basic sanitation
Brazil	4 007 240	38 068 780
Chile	176 200	176 200
Colombia	4 348 890	9 664 200
Costa Rica	146 160	292 320
Ecuador	2 203 320	2 675 460
Guatemala	928 080	3 093 600
Mexico	6 116 600	18 349 800
Peru	3 948 880	8 201 520
Botswana	45 168 480	71 516 760
Ethiopia	3 367 650	22 278 300
Ghana	16 854 520	31 047 800
Kenya	5 049 660	11 935 560
Mali	13 175 340	20 408 860
Nigeria	62 501 400	125 002 800
Rwanda	3 415 330	4 239 720
South Africa	2 638 800	13 721 760
Tanzania	23 148 910	43 342 640
Zambia	9 394 750	24 802 140
Zimbabwe	5 379 430	8 287 230
Egypt	820 560	3 282 240
Iran	3 097 880	8 519 170
Turkey	0	6 743 970
Bangladesh	23 489 250	67 335 850
China	111 466 960	487 667 950
India	87 649 800	801 369 600
Indonesia	37 479 900	102 445 060
Malaysia	3 335 640	17 512 110
Nepal	16 392 870	94 714 360
Pakistan	7 871 520	25 582 440
Philippines	2 680 400	4 690 700
Thailand	4 584 000	22 920 000

2012 data from WHO

THE NOBEL LAUREATES' GUIDE TO THE SMARTEST TARGETS FOR THE WORLD

Finn Kydland, *Nobel Laureate and Professor, University of California, Santa Barbara*
Tom Schelling, *Nobel Laureate and Professor, University of Maryland*
Nancy Stokey, *Professor, University of Chicago*

By September, the world's 193 governments will meet in New York and agree on a set of ambitious, global targets for 2030. Over the next 15 years these targets will direct the $2.5 trillion to be spent on development assistance, as well as countless trillions in national budgets.

Based on peer-reviewed analyses from 82 of the world's top economists and 44 sector experts organized by the Copenhagen Consensus, we have prioritized more than a hundred of the proposed targets in terms of their value-for-money. They are certainly not all equal. Some targets generate much higher economic, social and environmental benefits than others, per dollar spent.

The natural political inclination is to promise all good things to everyone, and the UN is currently poised to pick 169 well-intentioned targets. But the evidence at hand, although limited, indicates pretty clearly that some of these targets are much more promising than others. The analyses of the experts suggest that some of the targets are barely worthwhile, producing only a little more than $1 in social benefits per dollar spent, while others produce much higher social returns.

We have selected the 19 targets that we expect to produce the greatest benefits. The expert analyses suggest that if the UN concentrates on these top 19 targets, it can get $20 to $40 in social benefits per dollar spent, while allocating it evenly across all 169 targets would reduce the figure to less than $10. Being smart about spending could be better than doubling or quadrupling the aid budget. Our short list covers a lot of ground, but the thread that connects the individual targets is the benefits they will provide for people around the world in terms of health, the environment, and economic well-being, the three headings the UN has dubbed "people, planet and prosperity."

PEOPLE
- Lower chronic child malnutrition by 40%
- Halve malaria infection
- Reduce tuberculosis deaths by 90%
- Avoid 1.1 million HIV infections through circumcision
- Cut early death from chronic diseases by 1/3
- Reduce newborn mortality by 70%
- Increase immunization to reduce child deaths by 25%
- Make family planning available to everyone
- Eliminate violence against women and girls

PLANET
- Phase out fossil fuel subsidies
- Halve coral reef loss
- Tax pollution damage from energy
- Cut indoor air pollution by 20%

PROSPERITY
- Reduce trade restrictions (full Doha)
- Improve gender equality in ownership, business and politics
- Boost agricultural yield increase by 40%
- Increase girls' education by 2 years
- Achieve universal primary education in sub-Saharan Africa
- Triple preschool in sub-Saharan Africa

Consider a couple of targets that help people directly through health benefits. Tuberculosis (TB) is a 'hidden' disease. Over two billion people carry the bacterium that causes it, about 10% of those people will develop TB at some point, and about 1.5 million people each year die from TB. But treatment is inexpensive and, in most cases, highly effective. Spending a dollar on diagnosis and treatment is a low-cost way to give many more years of productive life to many people. Ebola may get the headlines, but TB is a much bigger problem.

Reducing childhood malnutrition is another excellent target. People of every age deserve to be well nourished, but nutrition is especially critical for young children. A good diet allows their brains and muscles to develop better, producing life-long benefits. Well-nourished children stay in school longer, learn more and end up being much more productive members of society. The available evidence suggests that providing better nutrition for 68 million children each year would produce over $40 in long-term social benefits for every dollar spent.

There are excellent targets involving the planet as well. Governments around the world still subsidize the use of fossil fuels to the tune of over $500bn each year. Cutting these subsidies would reduce pollution and free up resources for investments in health, education, and infrastructure. Protecting coral reefs turns out to be a surprisingly efficient target as well. There are benefits in terms of biodiversity, but healthy reefs also produce more tangible and immediate benefits. They increase fish stocks – benefitting both fishermen and consumers, and attract visitors who explore their beauties – benefitting everyone working in the tourist industry, as well as the tourists themselves.

Perhaps the most important, over-arching problem facing the world is poverty, which still afflicts billions of people. Poverty is the ultimate source of many other problems. Poor families have trouble providing their children with adequate food, education, and medical care. The immediate result is high rates of infant mortality, as well as poor cognitive skills and reduced productive capacity among surviving children. The ultimate result is a cycle of poverty.

Better nutrition and better schools will help alleviate poverty, but there is another target that promises to be even more effective: lowering barriers to international trade. The historical evidence on this point is compelling. In China, South Korea, India, Chile and many other countries, reducing trade restrictions has lifted incomes and reduced poverty, and triggered decades of rapid income growth. Poverty reduction was the first item in UN's list of Millennium Development Goals, and the numerical target was achieved. Why? Income growth in China was a big part of the story. And how did the Chinese achieve that remarkable feat? Most evidence suggests that international trade was a key ingredient. Trade produces immediate benefits by opening up markets, but it also facilitates the flow of ideas and technologies, producing even greater benefits over a longer horizon. A successful Doha free trade agreement could lift 160 million people out of extreme poverty.

Our list of targets will not solve all the world's problems, but neither can any list under realistic budgets. Our list can help the UN make its choices like a savvy shopper with limited funds. Choosing good targets will vastly increase the benefits to people around the world, as well as generations to come. Governments should forgo the instant gratification of promising everything to everyone, and instead focus on choosing smart development goals.

SMART DEVELOPMENT GOALS

Finn Kydland, *Nobel Laureate and Professor, University of California, Santa Barbara*
Tom Schelling, *Nobel Laureate and Professor, University of Maryland*
Nancy Stokey, *Professor, University of Chicago*

Over the course of 2014 and 2015, more than a hundred researchers evaluated the social, environmental and economic costs and benefits of more than 100 targets proposed by sector experts - economists, NGOs, UN agencies and businesses – across 22 topic areas. The topic areas were drawn from the High Level Panel and covered: air pollution, biodiversity, climate change, conflict and violence, data for development, energy, education, food security, nutrition, gender equality, governance and institutions, health systems, illicit financial flows, infant mortality and women's health, infectious diseases, infrastructure, non-communicable diseases, population and demography, poverty, science and technology, trade, and water and sanitation.

The expert panel has reviewed all this research and finds that the following 19 targets represent the best value-for-money in development over the period 2016 to 2030. The targets have been grouped into three broad themes: people, planet and prosperity echoing the UN's focus on social, environmental and economic pillars of development. The panel recognises that the elimination of extreme poverty remains an important, focal aspiration for the entire post-2015 agenda. Many of the targets below would help achieve reductions in poverty such as more free trade, educating pre-schoolers in Africa, nutrition and ensuring greater gender equality for women.

The expert panel find that reaching these global targets by 2030 would return more than $15 of good for every dollar spent benefitting people, planet and prosperity.

PEOPLE

Lower chronic child malnutrition by 40%

> Providing nutritional supplements, deworming, and improving the balance of diet for 0-2 year olds will cost $11bn and prevent 68m children from being malnourished every year

Halve malaria infection

> Distributing long lasting insecticide treated bed-nets and delaying resistance to the malaria drug artemisinin will cost $0.6bn, prevent 100m cases of malaria and save 440,000 lives per year

Reduce tuberculosis deaths by 90%

> Massively scaling up detection and treatment of tuberculosis will cost $8bn and save up to an additional 1.3m lives per year

Avoid 1.1 million HIV infections through circumcision

> Circumcising 90% of HIV-negative men in the 5 worst affected countries will cost $35m annually and avert 1.1m infections by 2030 with the preventive benefit increasing over time

Cut early death from chronic disease by 1/3

> Raising the price of tobacco, administering aspirin and preventative therapy for heart disease, reducing salt intake and providing low cost blood pressure medicine will cost $9bn and save 5m lives per year

Reduce newborn mortality by 70%

> Protecting expecting mothers from disease, having skilled medical staff support their deliveries, and ensuring high quality postnatal care will cost $14bn and prevent 2m newborn deaths per year

Eliminate violence against women and girls

> Right now, every year 305 million women are domestically abused, costing the world $4.4 trillion in damages

Increase immunization to reduce child deaths by 25%

> Expanding immunization coverage to include protection from forms of influenza, pneumonia and diarrheal disease will cost $1bn and save 1m children per year

Make family planning available to everyone

> Allowing women to decide if, when, and how often they become pregnant will cost $3.6bn per year, cut maternal deaths by 150,000, while providing a demographic dividend

PLANET

Phase out fossil fuel subsidies

> Removing fossil fuel subsidies will cost less than $37bn per year, lower carbon emissions and free up $548bn in government revenue to spend on for example, health, infrastructure and education

Halve coral reef loss

> Protecting marine habitats will cost $3bn per year but will prevent the loss of 3m hectares of coral reef, providing natural fishing hatcheries and boosting tourism

Tax pollution damage from energy

> Air pollution is the world's biggest environmental killer, causing more than 7m annual deaths. Taxes proportional to the damage from air pollution and CO_2 will reduce environmental impacts efficiently.

Cut indoor air pollution by 20%

> Providing more clean cookstoves will cost $11bn and prevent 1.3m deaths per year from indoor air pollution

PROSPERITY

Reduce trade restrictions (full Doha)

> Achieving more free trade (e.g. the Doha round) would make each person in the developing world $1,000 richer per year by 2030, lifting 160m people out of extreme poverty at a cost of $20bn per year

Improve gender equality in ownership, business and politics

> Ensuring women can own and inherit property, perform basic business needs like signing a contract and be represented in parliament will empower women

Boost agricultural yield growth by 40%

> Investing an extra $2.5bn per year in agricultural R&D to boost yields will reduce food prices for poor people, mean 80m fewer people go hungry and provide benefits worth $84bn per year

Increase girls' education by two years

> Ensuring girls receive more education will increase their future wages, improve their health, reduce their risk of violence and start a virtuous cycle for the next generations

Achieve universal primary education in sub-Saharan Africa

> At a cost of $9bn per year, this target will ensure 30m more kids per year attend primary school

Triple preschool in sub-Saharan Africa

> Pre-school instils within children a lifelong desire to learn. Ensuring pre-school coverage rises from 18% to 59% will cost up to $6bn and will give that experience to at least 30m more children per year

Youth Forums

The Youth Forums are a platform for young people to present their views on development priorities for the world to their national governments, the decision makers at the UN and the media.

Youth Forum participants learn from some of the world's leading economists about the social, economic and environmental benefits and costs of the many different targets being negotiated in the UN – covering education, gender, nutrition, health, violence, biodiversity, energy and more.

Their task as participants is to read about all the academic research papers described in this book. They then discuss and debate how much good the proposed targets would do for the world over the next 15 years and compare it to their costs.

Guided by these discussions and the economic evidence of costs and benefits, each participant rates the proposed targets as phenomenal, great, fair, poor or uncertain (see page 119) – exactly the same task as we asked of our Nobel Laureate Expert Panel.

Youth Forums are being organized across the Global South. Here are some examples of Youth Priorities (you can see many more pictures of top best and worst targets at instagram.com/post2015_ccc):

Enhance female education
Increase protected areas
Carla from Ecuador

Open world markets
Provide legal identity for all
Maria Jose Gellibert from Ecuador

Reduce child malnutrition
Increase birth rates in rich countries
Oyeladun Tayo S. from Nigeria

Open world markets for food and textiles
Give public pension for young-old ages
Mugizi Martin from Uganda

Gender equality
Edith from Kenya

Health
Climate change
Nyirarukundo Amira from Rwanda

Tripling pre-school in Sub-Saharan Africa
Data collection for all 169 targets
Jane Zulu from Zambia

Education
Alexander Shimpurt Soria from Peru

Free trade
Geronimo Vega Bora from Peru

Conflict and violence
Joel Quansah from Ghana

100% primary education in Sub-Saharan Africa
open world markets for food and textiles
Sosthenes Julius from Tanzania

GHANAIAN YOUTH SUGGEST DRASTIC REDUCTION IN WORLD IMPROVEMENT TARGETS

Published in the Daily Graphic, *the most widely read newspaper in Ghana, March 21st 2015*

In September, all 193 governments will announce a set of targets to improve the world between now and 2030. Now young people from Ghana, at youth fora discussing the post-2015 development agenda in Accra, have decided what they think should be at the top of the global priority list.

They have read and discussed research from 82 of the world's top economists and 44 sector experts organized by the Copenhagen Consensus with the help of the Youth Bridge Foundation, and prioritized which targets attain the most value for money.

Their assessments are really needed, because the older generation of UN ambassadors still have an implausibly long list of 169 targets, and not all of these targets are great. Some targets generate high economic, social and environmental benefits for their costs, while some cost a fortune while doing little good. It is appropriate that young people should help guide the final choice of priority targets, because it is their future.

Many major challenges are particularly acute in Africa, and so it is not surprising that the Ghanaian youth focused on some of these regional realities. In total, the youths of Ghana chose not 169 targets but said a much smaller set of 14 were the most important ones for the world.

The problems of violence featured several times in their list of top priorities. The economists writing the lead study on this issue showed that interpersonal violence has the greatest impact. Globally, nine people die through interpersonal violence – much of it domestic – for every person killed on the battlefield.

There is evidence that spending a cedi on targeted programs to reduce excessive alcohol consumption can pay back 17 cedi worth of benefits in terms of lower violence. At the same time, it will make people feel safer. That is part of the reason the young people of Ghana agreed that "reducing assaults" is one target the international community should adopt.

But assaults out in the community are a relatively minor problem compared to violence in the home or involving a close relative.

In sub-Saharan Africa, 125 million children each month are seriously abused. Not surprisingly, the youth forum said "ending violence in child discipline" was also a top priority. About a quarter of primary caregivers in Africa use severe physical punishment and, in addition to the injuries and psychological damage inflicted on children, this has real economic costs. Spending a cedi on this program would give benefits worth 10 cedi.

The youth forum also picked "women's reproductive health" as one of the world's important priorities. The economists give them a lot of reason to do so; by allowing them to control the number and timing of their children, mothers would be better able to cope with the children they do have and the children themselves would be better fed and educated. This has huge benefits, valued at 120 cedi for each one spent.

There were also other priorities on health. The youngsters picked malaria and TB as crucial targets for the world community. Dealing with malaria is both doable and very cost-effective. Use of insecticide-treated bed nets to prevent mosquitoes biting and spreading malaria plus treating any cases which do occur with an effective combination of drugs would pay back 36 cedi for each one the program cost. Diagnosing and treating TB is an even better investment; every cedi spent would give 43 cedi worth of benefits.

They also picked a key nutrition target. Far too many children in the region are undernourished, particularly in the crucial first 1,000 days from conception through to age two. Their physical and mental development suffers, they do less well at school and earn less throughout their lives. Providing nutritional supplements to infants boosts household incomes by two-thirds by the time they are adults. A cedi spent on this pays back 18 cedi of benefits.

Young people also care about the planet. They put reducing the loss of forests high on their list of priorities, to retain biodiversity and natural capital more generally. This is also a really good investment, with each cedi spent giving 10 cedi worth of benefits.

But perhaps most importantly, the youth emphasized that poverty is at the root of many of these problems. People struggling to live day to day can't afford enough nutritious food or good healthcare and often suffer most from violence. That's why the young Ghanaians put "eliminate extreme poverty" as one of the top targets to focus on. Not only would this transform people's lives, but spending one cedi to do so would pay back five in social benefits.

Making such a prioritization is brave of these young men and women, both because it is hard, but also because it is necessary to show what is most important. It is, after all, their future. I look forward to taking their list, along with those from other youth forums from Africa, Asia and Latin America to the United Nations in New York, to help the ambassadors make better choices.

Appendix

THE UN'S 169 TARGETS EVALUATED

Over the next pages you can read the UN's 169 targets. They are the conclusion of the so-called Open Working Group, which involved over 90 nations meeting 23 times over two years.

But you're not just reading the words of the many UN ambassadors. There is also a color-coding indicating how effective each target is.

We arrived at the color by asking 32 of the world's top economists in their respective fields to provide an informed estimate of the economic costs and benefits associated with the strategies that would be available to implement the 169 targets. You can read much more about the participants, the evaluation, their estimates, the academic explanations and suggestions for how a better wording would make the target more effective at http://bit.ly/1plSApx.

While costs and benefits are considered in dollars, this is not just about money. Economic, social and environmental benefits have been assessed and the ratings are based on the monetized conversion of all three factors.

The color-coding is:

PHENOMENAL – Robust evidence for benefits more than 15 times higher than costs

GOOD – Robust evidence of benefits between 5 to 15 times higher than costs

FAIR – Robust evidence of benefits between 1 to 5 times higher than costs

POOR – The benefits are smaller than costs or target poorly specified (e.g. internally inconsistent, incentivizes wrong activity)

UNCERTAIN – There is not enough knowledge of the policy options that could reach the target or the costs and benefits of the actions to reach the target are not well known

So take target 3.3. The economist marked it up like this:

3.3 by 2030 end the epidemics of AIDS, tuberculosis, malaria, and neglected tropical diseases and combat hepatitis, water-borne diseases, and other communicable diseases

The economists tell us that as written this target is **POOR**, because the ambition of ending these diseases by 2030 is unrealistic. However, achieving realistic reductions in the burden of these diseases is possible, and has the following ratings: HIV/AIDS **FAIR,** tuberculosis **PHENOMENAL**, malaria **PHENOMENAL** (Jamison et al, 2012) and neglected tropic diseases, **PHENOMENAL** (Musgrove and Hotez, 2009) hepatitis **UNCERTAIN** (potentially even **POOR**) because the studies are old (Tepakdee et al. 2002), water-borne diseases is **GOOD** (Hutton and Haller, 2004) and other communicable diseases is **UNCERTAIN** because the concept is too broad to be sure.

The economists go on to suggest other and better targets, like the final target on tuberculosis: "Reduce tuberculosis deaths by 90%."

Legend: **PHENOMENAL** **GOOD** **FAIR** **POOR** **UNCERTAIN**

The Open Working Group's Proposal for Sustainable Development Goals

Proposed goal 1. End poverty in all its forms everywhere

1.1　by 2030, eradicate extreme poverty for all people everywhere, currently measured as people living on less than $1.25 a day

1.2　by 2030, reduce at least by half the proportion of men, women and children of all ages living in poverty in all its dimensions according to national definitions

1.3　implement nationally appropriate social protection systems and measures for all, including floors, and by 2030 achieve substantial coverage of the poor and the vulnerable

1.4　by 2030 ensure that all men and women, particularly the poor and the vulnerable, have equal rights to economic resources, as well as access to basic services, ownership, and control over land and other forms of property, inheritance, natural resources, appropriate new technology, and financial services including microfinance

1.5　by 2030 build the resilience of the poor and those in vulnerable situations, and reduce their exposure and vulnerability to climate-related extreme events and other economic, social and environmental shocks and disasters

1.a　ensure significant mobilization of resources from a variety of sources, including through enhanced development cooperation to provide adequate and predictable means for developing countries, in particular LDCs, to implement programmes and policies to end poverty in all its dimensions

1.b　create sound policy frameworks, at national, regional and international levels, based on pro-poor and gender-sensitive development strategies to support accelerated investments in poverty eradication actions

Legend: **PHENOMENAL** GOOD FAIR POOR UNCERTAIN

Proposed goal 2. End hunger, achieve food security and improved nutrition, and promote sustainable agriculture

2.1 by 2030 end hunger and ensure access by all people, in particular the poor and people in vulnerable situations including infants, to safe, nutritious and sufficient food all year round

2.2 by 2030 end all forms of malnutrition, including achieving by 2025 the internationally agreed targets on stunting and wasting in children under five years of age, and address the nutritional needs of adolescent girls, pregnant and lactating women, and older persons

2.3 by 2030 double the agricultural productivity and the incomes of small-scale food producers, particularly women, indigenous peoples, family farmers, pastoralists and fishers, including through secure and equal access to land, other productive resources and inputs, knowledge, financial services, markets, and opportunities for value addition and non-farm employment

2.4 by 2030 ensure sustainable food production systems and implement resilient agricultural practices that increase productivity and production, that help maintain ecosystems, that strengthen capacity for adaptation to climate change, extreme weather, drought, flooding and other disasters, and that progressively improve land and soil quality

2.5 by 2020 maintain genetic diversity of seeds, cultivated plants, farmed and domesticated animals and their related wild species, including through soundly managed and diversified seed and plant banks at national, regional and international levels, and ensure access to and fair and equitable sharing of benefits arising from the utilization of genetic resources and associated traditional knowledge as internationally agreed

2.a increase investment, including through enhanced international cooperation, in rural infrastructure, agricultural research and extension services, technology development, and plant and livestock gene banks to enhance agricultural productive capacity in developing countries, in particular in least developed countries

Legend: **PHENOMENAL** GOOD FAIR POOR UNCERTAIN

2.b correct and prevent trade restrictions and distortions in world agricultural markets including the parallel elimination of all forms of agricultural export subsidies and all export measures with equivalent effect, in accordance with the mandate of the Doha Development Round

2.c adopt measures to ensure the proper functioning of food commodity markets and their derivatives, and facilitate timely access to market information, including on food reserves, in order to help limit extreme food price volatility

Proposed goal 3. Ensure healthy lives and promote well-being for all at all ages

3.1 by 2030 reduce the global maternal mortality ratio to less than 70 per 100,000 live births

3.2 by 2030 end preventable deaths of newborns and under-five children

3.3 by 2030 end the epidemics of AIDS, tuberculosis, malaria, and neglected tropical diseases and combat hepatitis, water-borne diseases, and other communicable diseases

3.4 by 2030 reduce by one-third pre-mature mortality from non-communicable diseases (NCDs) through prevention and treatment, and promote mental health and wellbeing

3.5 strengthen prevention and treatment of substance abuse, including narcotic drug abuse and harmful use of alcohol

3.6 by 2020 halve global deaths and injuries from road traffic accidents

3.7 by 2030 ensure universal access to sexual and reproductive health care services, including for family planning, information and education, and the integration of reproductive health into national strategies and programmes

Legend: **PHENOMENAL** **GOOD** **FAIR** **POOR** **UNCERTAIN**

3.8   achieve universal health coverage (UHC), including financial risk protection, access to quality essential health care services, and access to safe, effective, quality, and affordable essential medicines and vaccines for all

3.9   by 2030 substantially reduce the number of deaths and illnesses from hazardous chemicals and air, water, and soil pollution and contamination

3.a   strengthen implementation of the Framework Convention on Tobacco Control in all countries as appropriate

3.b   support research and development of vaccines and medicines for the communicable and non-communicable diseases that primarily affect developing countries, provide access to affordable essential medicines and vaccines, in accordance with the Doha Declaration which affirms the right of developing countries to use to the full the provisions in the TRIPS agreement regarding flexibilities to protect public health and, in particular, provide access to medicines for all

3.c   increase substantially health financing and the recruitment, development and training and retention of the health workforce in developing countries, especially in LDCs and SIDS

3.d   strengthen the capacity of all countries, particularly developing countries, for early warning, risk reduction, and management of national and global health risks

Proposed goal 4. Ensure inclusive and equitable quality education and promote life-long learning opportunities for all

4.1   by 2030, ensure that all girls and boys complete free, equitable and quality primary and secondary education leading to relevant and effective learning outcomes

4.2   by 2030 ensure that all girls and boys have access to quality early childhood development, care and pre-primary education so that they are ready for primary education

Legend: **PHENOMENAL** **GOOD** **FAIR** **POOR** **UNCERTAIN**

4.3 by 2030 ensure equal access for all women and men to affordable quality technical, vocational and tertiary education, including university

4.4 by 2030, increase by x% the number of youth and adults who have relevant skills, including technical and vocational skills, for employment, decent jobs and entrepreneurship

4.5 by 2030, eliminate gender disparities in education and ensure equal access to all levels of education and vocational training for the vulnerable, including persons with disabilities, indigenous peoples, and children in vulnerable situations

4.6 by 2030 ensure that all youth and at least x% of adults, both men and women, achieve literacy and numeracy

4.7 by 2030 ensure all learners acquire knowledge and skills needed to promote sustainable development, including among others through education for sustainable development and sustainable lifestyles, human rights, gender equality, promotion of a culture of peace and non-violence, global citizenship, and appreciation of cultural diversity and of culture's contribution to sustainable development

4.a build and upgrade education facilities that are child, disability and gender sensitive and provide safe, non-violent, inclusive and effective learning environments for all

4.b by 2020 expand by x% globally the number of scholarships for developing countries in particular LDCs, SIDS and African countries to enrol in higher education, including vocational training, ICT, technical, engineering and scientific programmes in developed countries and other developing countries

4.c by 2030 increase by x% the supply of qualified teachers, including through international cooperation for teacher training in developing countries, especially LDCs and SIDS

Legend: **PHENOMENAL** **GOOD** **FAIR** **POOR** **UNCERTAIN**

Proposed goal 5. Achieve gender equality and empower all women and girls

5.1 end all forms of discrimination against all women and girls everywhere

5.2 eliminate all forms of violence against all women and girls in public and private spheres, including trafficking and sexual and other types of exploitation

5.3 eliminate all harmful practices, such as child, early and forced marriage and female genital mutilations

5.4 recognize and value unpaid care and domestic work through the provision of public services, infrastructure and social protection policies, and the promotion of shared responsibility within the household and the family as nationally appropriate

5.5 ensure women's full and effective participation and equal opportunities for leadership at all levels of decision-making in political, economic, and public life

5.6 ensure universal access to sexual and reproductive health and reproductive rights as agreed in accordance with the Programme of Action of the ICPD and the Beijing Platform for Action and the outcome documents of their review conferences

5.a undertake reforms to give women equal rights to economic resources, as well as access to ownership and control over land and other forms of property, financial services, inheritance, and natural resources in accordance with national laws

5.b enhance the use of enabling technologies, in particular ICT, to promote women's empowerment

5.c adopt and strengthen sound policies and enforceable legislation for the promotion of gender equality and the empowerment of all women and girls at all levels

Proposed goal 6. Ensure availability and sustainable management of water and sanitation for all

6.1 by 2030, achieve universal and equitable access to safe and affordable drinking water for all

6.2 by 2030, achieve access to adequate and equitable sanitation and hygiene for all, and end open defecation, paying special attention to the needs of women and girls and those in vulnerable situations

6.3 by 2030, improve water quality by reducing pollution, eliminating dumping and minimizing release of hazardous chemicals and materials, halving the proportion of untreated wastewater, and increasing recycling and safe reuse by x% globally

6.4 by 2030, substantially increase water-use efficiency across all sectors and ensure sustainable withdrawals and supply of freshwater to address water scarcity, and substantially reduce the number of people suffering from water scarcity

6.5 by 2030 implement integrated water resources management at all levels, including through transboundary cooperation as appropriate

6.6 by 2020 protect and restore water-related ecosystems, including mountains, forests, wetlands, rivers, aquifers and lakes

6.a by 2030, expand international cooperation and capacity-building support to developing countries in water and sanitation related activities and programmes, including water harvesting, desalination, water efficiency, wastewater treatment, recycling and reuse technologies

6.b support and strengthen the participation of local communities for improving water and sanitation management

Legend: **PHENOMENAL** **GOOD** **FAIR** **POOR** **UNCERTAIN**

Proposed goal 7. Ensure access to affordable, reliable, sustainable, and modern energy for all

7.1 by 2030 ensure universal access to affordable, reliable, and modern energy services

7.2 increase substantially the share of renewable energy in the global energy mix by 2030

7.3 double the global rate of improvement in energy efficiency by 2030

7.a by 2030 enhance international cooperation to facilitate access to clean energy research and technologies, including renewable energy, energy efficiency, and advanced and cleaner fossil fuel technologies, and promote investment in energy infrastructure and clean energy technologies

7.b by 2030 expand infrastructure and upgrade technology for supplying modern and sustainable energy services for all in developing countries, particularly LDCs and SIDS

Proposed goal 8. Promote sustained, inclusive and sustainable economic growth, full and productive employment and decent work for all

8.1 sustain per capita economic growth in accordance with national circumstances, and in particular at least 7% per annum GDP growth in the least-developed countries

8.2 achieve higher levels of productivity of economies through diversification, technological upgrading and innovation, including through a focus on high value added and labour-intensive sectors

8.3 promote development-oriented policies that support productive activities, decent job creation, entrepreneurship, creativity and innovation, and encourage formalization and growth of micro-, small- and medium-sized enterprises in-

Legend: **PHENOMENAL** **GOOD** **FAIR** **POOR** **UNCERTAIN**

cluding through access to financial services

8.4 improve progressively through 2030 global resource efficiency in consumption and production, and endeavour to decouple economic growth from environmental degradation in accordance with the 10-year framework of programmes on sustainable consumption and production with developed countries taking the lead

8.5 by 2030 achieve full and productive employment and decent work for all women and men, including for young people and persons with disabilities, and equal pay for work of equal value

8.6 by 2020 substantially reduce the proportion of youth not in employment, education or training

8.7 take immediate and effective measures to secure the prohibition and elimination of the worst forms of child labour, eradicate forced labour, and by 2025 end child labour in all its forms including recruitment and use of child soldiers

8.8 protect labour rights and promote safe and secure working environments of all workers, including migrant workers, particularly women migrants, and those in precarious employment

8.9 by 2030 devise and implement policies to promote sustainable tourism which creates jobs, promotes local culture and products

8.10 strengthen the capacity of domestic financial institutions to encourage and to expand access to banking, insurance and financial services for all

8.a increase Aid for Trade support for developing countries, particularly LDCs, including through the Enhanced Integrated Framework for LDCs

8.b by 2020 develop and operationalize a global strategy for youth employment and implement the ILO Global Jobs Pact

Legend: **PHENOMENAL** **GOOD** **FAIR** **POOR** **UNCERTAIN**

Proposed goal 9. Build resilient infrastructure, promote inclusive and sustainable industrialization and foster innovation

9.1 develop quality, reliable, sustainable and resilient infrastructure, including regional and trans-border infrastructure, to support economic development and human well-being, with a focus on affordable and equitable access for all

9.2 promote inclusive and sustainable industrialization, and by 2030 raise significantly industry's share of employment and GDP in line with national circumstances, and double its share in LDCs

9.3 increase the access of small-scale industrial and other enterprises, particularly in developing countries, to financial services including affordable credit and their integration into value chains and markets

9.4 by 2030 upgrade infrastructure and retrofit industries to make them sustainable, with increased resource use efficiency and greater adoption of clean and environmentally sound technologies and industrial processes, all countries taking action in accordance with their respective capabilities

9.5 enhance scientific research, upgrade the technological capabilities of industrial sectors in all countries, particularly developing countries, including by 2030 encouraging innovation and increasing the number of R&D workers per one million people by x% and public and private R&D spending

9.a facilitate sustainable and resilient infrastructure development in developing countries through enhanced financial, technological and technical support to African countries, LDCs, LLDCs and SIDS

9.b support domestic technology development, research and innovation in developing countries including by ensuring a conducive policy environment for inter alia industrial diversification and value addition to commodities

9.c significantly increase access to ICT and strive to provide universal and affordable access to internet in LDCs by 2020

Legend: **PHENOMENAL** **GOOD** **FAIR** **POOR** UNCERTAIN

Proposed goal 10. Reduce inequality within and among countries

10.1 by 2030 progressively achieve and sustain income growth of the bottom 40% of the population at a rate higher than the national average

10.2 by 2030 empower and promote the social, economic and political inclusion of all irrespective of age, sex, disability, race, ethnicity, origin, religion or economic or other status

10.3 ensure equal opportunity and reduce inequalities of outcome, including through eliminating discriminatory laws, policies and practices and promoting appropriate legislation, policies and actions in this regard

10.4 adopt policies especially fiscal, wage, and social protection policies and progressively achieve greater equality

10.5 improve regulation and monitoring of global financial markets and institutions and strengthen implementation of such regulations

10.6 ensure enhanced representation and voice of developing countries in decision making in global international economic and financial institutions in order to deliver more effective, credible, accountable and legitimate institutions

10.7 facilitate orderly, safe, regular and responsible migration and mobility of people, including through implementation of planned and well-managed migration policies

10.a implement the principle of special and differential treatment for developing countries, in particular least developed countries, in accordance with WTO agreements

10.b encourage ODA and financial flows, including foreign direct investment, to states where the need is greatest, in particular LDCs, African countries, SIDS, and LLDCs, in accordance with their national plans and programmes

Legend: **PHENOMENAL** GOOD FAIR **POOR** UNCERTAIN

10.c by 2030, reduce to less than 3% the transaction costs of migrant remittances and eliminate remittance corridors with costs higher than 5%

Proposed goal 11. Make cities and human settlements inclusive, safe, resilient and sustainable

11.1 by 2030, ensure access for all to adequate, safe and affordable housing and basic services, and upgrade slums

11.2 by 2030, provide access to safe, affordable, accessible and sustainable transport systems for all, improving road safety, notably by expanding public transport, with special attention to the needs of those in vulnerable situations, women, children, persons with disabilities and older persons

11.3 by 2030 enhance inclusive and sustainable urbanization and capacities for participatory, integrated and sustainable human settlement planning and management in all countries

11.4 strengthen efforts to protect and safeguard the world's cultural and natural heritage

11.5 by 2030 significantly reduce the number of deaths and the number of affected people and decrease by y% the economic losses relative to GDP caused by disasters, including water-related disasters, with the focus on protecting the poor and people in vulnerable situations

11.6 by 2030, reduce the adverse per capita environmental impact of cities, including by paying special attention to air quality, municipal and other waste management

11.7 by 2030, provide universal access to safe, inclusive and accessible, green and public spaces, particularly for women and children, older persons and persons with disabilities

11.a support positive economic, social and environmental links between urban, peri-urban and rural areas by strengthening national and regional development planning

Legend: **PHENOMENAL** GOOD FAIR POOR UNCERTAIN

11.b by 2020, increase by x% the number of cities and human settlements adopting and implementing integrated policies and plans towards inclusion, resource efficiency, mitigation and adaptation to climate change, resilience to disasters, develop and implement in line with the forthcoming Hyogo Framework holistic disaster risk management at all levels

11.c support least developed countries, including through financial and technical assistance, for sustainable and resilient buildings utilizing local materials

Proposed goal 12. Ensure sustainable consumption and production patterns

12.1 implement the 10-Year Framework of Programmes on sustainable consumption and production (10YFP), all countries taking action, with developed countries taking the lead, taking into account the development and capabilities of developing countries

12.2 by 2030 achieve sustainable management and efficient use of natural resources

12.3 by 2030 halve per capita global food waste at the retail and consumer level, and reduce food losses along production and supply chains including post-harvest losses

12.4 by 2020 achieve environmentally sound management of chemicals and all wastes throughout their life cycle in accordance with agreed international frameworks and significantly reduce their release to air, water and soil to minimize their adverse impacts on human health and the environment

12.5 by 2030, substantially reduce waste generation through prevention, reduction, recycling, and reuse

12.6 encourage companies, especially large and trans-national companies, to adopt sustainable practices and to integrate sustainability information into their reporting cycle

Legend: **PHENOMENAL** **GOOD** **FAIR** **POOR** UNCERTAIN

12.7 promote public procurement practices that are sustainable in accordance with national policies and priorities

12.8 by 2030 ensure that people everywhere have the relevant information and awareness for sustainable development and lifestyles in harmony with nature

12.a support developing countries to strengthen their scientific and technological capacities to move towards more sustainable patterns of consumption and production

12.b develop and implement tools to monitor sustainable development impacts for sustainable tourism which creates jobs, promotes local culture and products

12.c rationalize inefficient fossil fuel subsidies that encourage wasteful consumption by removing market distortions, in accordance with national circumstances, including by restructuring taxation and phasing out those harmful subsidies, where they exist, to reflect their environmental impacts, taking fully into account the specific needs and conditions of developing countries and minimizing the possible adverse impacts on their development in a manner that protects the poor and the affected communities

Proposed goal 13. Take urgent action to combat climate change and its impacts*

> *Acknowledging that the UNFCCC is the primary international, intergovernmental forum for negotiating the global response to climate change.

13.1 strengthen resilience and adaptive capacity to climate related hazards and natural disasters in all countries

13.2 integrate climate change measures into national policies, strategies, and planning

13.3 improve education, awareness raising and human and institutional capacity on climate change mitigation, adaptation, impact reduction, and early warning

134

Legend: **PHENOMENAL** **GOOD** **FAIR** **POOR** UNCERTAIN

13.a implement the commitment undertaken by developed country Parties to the UNFCCC to a goal of mobilizing jointly USD100 billion annually by 2020 from all sources to address the needs of developing countries in the context of meaningful mitigation actions and transparency on implementation and fully operationalize the Green Climate Fund through its capitalization as soon as possible

13.b Promote mechanisms for raising capacities for effective climate change related planning and management, in LDCs, including focusing on women, youth, local and marginalized communities

Proposed goal 14. Conserve and sustainably use the oceans, seas and marine resources for sustainable development

14.1 by 2025, prevent and significantly reduce marine pollution of all kinds, particularly from land-based activities, including marine debris and nutrient pollution

14.2 by 2020, sustainably manage and protect marine and coastal ecosystems to avoid significant adverse impacts, including by strengthening their resilience, and take action for their restoration, to achieve healthy and productive oceans

14.3 minimize and address the impacts of ocean acidification, including through enhanced scientific cooperation at all levels

14.4 by 2020, effectively regulate harvesting, and end overfishing, illegal, unreported and unregulated (IUU) fishing and destructive fishing practices and implement science-based management plans, to restore fish stocks in the shortest time feasible at least to levels that can produce maximum sustainable yield as determined by their biological characteristics

14.5 by 2020, conserve at least 10 per cent of coastal and marine

Legend: <mark style="background:lightgreen">PHENOMENAL</mark> <mark style="background:palegreen">GOOD</mark> <mark style="background:yellow">FAIR</mark> <mark style="background:orangered">POOR</mark> UNCERTAIN

<mark style="background:yellow">areas, consistent with national and international law and based on best available scientific information</mark>

14.6 <mark style="background:lightgreen">by 2020, prohibit certain forms of fisheries subsidies which contribute to overcapacity and overfishing, and eliminate subsidies that contribute to IUU fishing, and refrain from introducing new such subsidies, recognizing that appropriate and effective special and differential treatment for developing and least developed countries should be an integral part of the WTO fisheries subsidies negotiation[1]</mark>

14.7 <mark style="background:lightgreen">by 2030 increase the economic benefits to SIDS and LDCs from the sustainable use of marine resources, including through sustainable management of fisheries,</mark> aquaculture and tourism

14.a increase scientific knowledge, develop research capacities and transfer marine technology taking into account the Intergovernmental Oceanographic Commission Criteria and Guidelines on the Transfer of Marine Technology, in order to improve ocean health and to enhance the contribution of marine biodiversity to the development of developing countries, in particular SIDS and LDCs

14.b <mark style="background:yellow">provide access of small-scale artisanal fishers to marine resources and markets</mark>

14.c <mark style="background:yellow">ensure the full implementation of international law, as reflected in UNCLOS for states parties to it, including, where applicable, existing regional and international regimes for the conservation and sustainable use of oceans and their resources by their parties</mark>

---

1 Taking into account ongoing WTO negotiations and WTO Doha Development Agenda and Hong Kong Ministerial Mandate.

Legend: <mark style="background:#4caf50">PHENOMENAL</mark> <mark style="background:#c8e6c9">GOOD</mark> <mark style="background:#fff59d">FAIR</mark> <mark style="background:#ff7043">POOR</mark> UNCERTAIN

Proposed goal 15. Protect, restore and promote sustainable use of terrestrial ecosystems, sustainably manage forests, combat desertification, and halt and reverse land degradation and halt biodiversity loss

15.1 <mark style="background:#c8e6c9">by 2020 ensure conservation, restoration and sustainable use of terrestrial and inland freshwater ecosystems and their services, in particular forests, wetlands, mountains and drylands, in line with obligations under international agreements</mark>

15.2 <mark style="background:#c8e6c9">by 2020, promote the implementation of sustainable management of all types of forests, halt deforestation, restore degraded forests, and increase afforestation and reforestation by x% globally</mark>

15.3 by 2020, combat desertification, and restore degraded land and soil, including land affected by desertification, drought and floods, and strive to achieve a land-degradation neutral world

15.4 by 2030 ensure the conservation of mountain ecosystems, including their biodiversity, to enhance their capacity to provide benefits which are essential for sustainable development

15.5 take urgent and significant action to reduce degradation of natural habitat, halt the loss of biodiversity, and by 2020 protect and prevent the extinction of threatened species

15.6 ensure fair and equitable sharing of the benefits arising from the utilization of genetic resources, and promote appropriate access to genetic resources

15.7 <mark style="background:#fff59d">take urgent action to end poaching and trafficking of protected species of flora and fauna, and address both demand and supply of illegal wildlife products</mark>

15.8 <mark style="background:#fff59d">by 2020 introduce measures to prevent the introduction and significantly reduce the impact of invasive alien species on land and water ecosystems, and control or eradicate the priority species</mark>

Legend: **PHENOMENAL** **GOOD** **FAIR** **POOR** UNCERTAIN

15.9 <mark>by 2020, integrate ecosystems and biodiversity values into national and local planning, development processes and poverty reduction strategies, and accounts</mark>

15.a mobilize and significantly increase from all sources financial resources to conserve and sustainably use biodiversity and ecosystems

15.b mobilize significantly resources from all sources and at all levels to finance sustainable forest management, and provide adequate incentives to developing countries to advance sustainable forest management, including for conservation and reforestation

15.c <mark>enhance global support to efforts to combat poaching and trafficking of protected species, including by increasing the capacity of local communities to pursue sustainable livelihood opportunities</mark>

Proposed Goal 16. Promote peaceful and inclusive societies for sustainable development, provide access to justice for all and build effective, accountable and inclusive institutions at all levels

16.1 significantly reduce all forms of violence and related death rates everywhere

16.2 end abuse, exploitation, trafficking and all forms of violence and torture against children

16.3 promote the rule of law at the national and international levels, and ensure equal access to justice for all

16.4 <mark>by 2030 significantly reduce illicit financial</mark> and arms flows, strengthen recovery and return of stolen assets, and combat all forms of organized crime

16.5 substantially reduce corruption and bribery in all its forms

Legend: **PHENOMENAL** **GOOD** **FAIR** **POOR** UNCERTAIN

16.6 develop effective, accountable and transparent institutions at all levels

16.7 ensure responsive, inclusive, participatory and representative decision-making at all levels

16.8 broaden and strengthen the participation of developing countries in the institutions of global governance

16.9 by 2030 provide legal identity for all including birth registration

16.10 ensure public access to information and protect fundamental freedoms, in accordance with national legislation and international agreements

16.a strengthen relevant national institutions, including through international cooperation, for building capacities at all levels, in particular in developing countries, for preventing violence and combating terrorism and crime

16.b promote and enforce non-discriminatory laws and policies for sustainable development

Proposed goal 17. Strengthen the means of implementation and revitalize the global partnership for sustainable development

Finance

17.1 strengthen domestic resource mobilization, including through international support to developing countries to improve domestic capacity for tax and other revenue collection

17.2 developed countries to implement fully their ODA commitments, including to provide 0.7% of GNI in ODA to developing countries of which 0.15-0.20% to least-developed countries

17.3 mobilize additional financial resources for developing countries from multiple sources

Legend: **PHENOMENAL** **GOOD** **FAIR** **POOR** UNCERTAIN

17.4 assist developing countries in attaining long-term debt sustainability through coordinated policies aimed at fostering debt financing, debt relief and debt restructuring, as appropriate, and address the external debt of highly indebted poor countries (HIPC) to reduce debt distress

17.5 adopt and implement investment promotion regimes for LDCs

Technology

17.6 enhance North-South, South-South and triangular regional and international cooperation on and access to science, technology and innovation, and enhance knowledge sharing on mutually agreed terms, including through improved coordination among existing mechanisms, particularly at UN level, and through a global technology facilitation mechanism when agreed

17.7 promote development, transfer, dissemination and diffusion of environmentally sound technologies to developing countries on favourable terms, including on concessional and preferential terms, as mutually agreed

17.8 fully operationalize the Technology Bank and STI (Science, Technology and Innovation) capacity building mechanism for LDCs by 2017, and enhance the use of enabling technologies in particular ICT

Capacity building

17.9 enhance international support for implementing effective and targeted capacity building in developing countries to support national plans to implement all sustainable development goals, including through North-South, South-South, and triangular cooperation

Legend: **PHENOMENAL** **GOOD** **FAIR** **POOR** **UNCERTAIN**

Trade

17.10 promote a universal, rules-based, open, non-discriminatory and equitable multilateral trading system under the WTO including through the conclusion of negotiations within its Doha Development Agenda

17.11 increase significantly the exports of developing countries, in particular with a view to doubling the LDC share of global exports by 2020

17.12 realize timely implementation of duty-free, quota-free market access on a lasting basis for all least developed countries consistent with WTO decisions, including through ensuring that preferential rules of origin applicable to imports from LDCs are transparent and simple, and contribute to facilitating market access

Systemic issues

Policy and institutional coherence

17.13 enhance global macroeconomic stability including through policy coordination and policy coherence

17.14 enhance policy coherence for sustainable development

17.15 respect each country's policy space and leadership to establish and implement policies for poverty eradication and sustainable development

Multi-stakeholder partnerships

17.16 enhance the global partnership for sustainable development complemented by multi- stakeholder partnerships that mobilize and share knowledge, expertise, technologies and financial resources to support the achievement of sustainable development goals in all countries, particularly developing countries

Legend: **PHENOMENAL** **GOOD** **FAIR** **POOR** **UNCERTAIN**

17.17 encourage and promote effective public, public-private, and civil society partnerships, building on the experience and re-sourcing strategies of partnerships

Data, monitoring and accountability

17.18 by 2020, enhance capacity building support to developing countries, including for LDCs and SIDS, to increase significantly the availability of high-quality, timely and reliable data disaggregated by income, gender, age, race, ethnicity, migratory status, disability, geographic location and other characteristics relevant in national contexts

17.19 by 2030, build on existing initiatives to develop measurements of progress on sustainable development that complement GDP, and support statistical capacity building in developing countries

SUGGESTED FURTHER READING ON POST-2015 CONSENSUS

At the UN, a free Free-for-All on Setting Global Goals, *New York Times,* May 6. 2015

Smart Aid for the World's Poor, *Wall Street Journal,* July 25. 2014

Violence between individuals 'kills nine times more people' than wars, *The Guardian,* September 9. 2014

How to Make the World's Poor $500 Billion Richer, *TIME,* September 17. 2014

Visas Best Bet to Strengthen Technology in Developing Countries, *Wall Street Journal,* September 19. 2014

World risks spending $250 billion just to monitor U.N. development goals, *Reuters,* September 24. 2014

More or Better Development Data? Yes, Please..., *Huffington Post,* October 8. 2014

How Indoor Stoves Can Help Solve Global Poverty, *TIME,* October 3. 2014

Feeding people is smart: It's the best investment to do good in the world, *Economic Times India,* October 16. 2014

WTO Doha deal would make world $11-trillion richer by 2030, *AFP,* October 21. 2014

Fixing the World, Bang-for-the-Buck Edition, *Feakonomics radio podcast,* November 2. 2014

Promises to Keep, Crafting Better Development Goals, *Foreign Affairs,* November/December issue 2014

The United Nations needs a shorter, stronger game plan for humanity, *Washington Post,* November 21. 2014

United Nations debates new goals for making world a better place, *Sydney Morning Herald,* December 5. 2014

The economics of optimism, *The Economist,* January 22. 2015

Better Infrastructure Would Cut Food Waste, *Wall Street Journal*, February 22. 2015

The spread of western disease: 'The poor are dying more and more like the rich', *The Guardian*, March 2. 2015

The good, the bad and the hideous, *The Economist*, March 26. 2015

Limit UN development goals for 2030, get more value for money, *Reuters*, March 26. 2015

Articles on Post-2015 Consensus research and outcome have been published in Albania, Argentina, Australia, Bahrain, Bangladesh, Belgium, Bolivia, Brazil, Cambodia, Canada, Chile, China, Colombia, Costa Rica, Croatia, Cuba, Cyprus, Czech Republic, Denmark, Dominican Republic, Ecuador, Egypt, El Salvador, Estonia, Ethiopia, Finland, France, Germany, Ghana, Greece, Guatemala, Guyana, Honduras, Hungary, India, Indonesia, Ireland, Italy, Japan, Kenya, Kosovo, Lebanon, Malaysia, Mali, Malta, Mexico, Mozambique, Namibia, Nepal, New Zealand, Nicaragua, Nigeria, Norway, Oman, Pakistan, Panamá, Peru, Philippines, Poland, Portugal, Qatar, Russia, Rwanda, Saudi Arabia, Singapore, Somalia, South Africa, South Korea, Spain, Sri Lanka, Sweden, Switzerland, Thailand, Turkey, Uganda, United Arab Emirates, United Kingdom, United States, Uruguay, Venezuela, Vietnam and Zimbabwe.